The Ultimate Small Business
Owner's Guide:
5 Simple Secrets to Attracting More
Customers, Keeping Customers for Life
And Striking Gold with Your Bottom Line

Elton Pride

The Ultimate Small Business Owner's Guide:
5 Simple Secrets to Attracting More Customers, Keeping
Customers for Life And Striking Gold with Your Bottom Line

Copyright © 2013 by Elton Pride

ISBN 10: 0-9848462-4-7
ISBN 13: 978-0-9848462-4-5

Published by: Expert Author Publishing
http://expertauthorpublishing.com

Canadian Address
1265 Charter Hill Drive
Coquitlam, BC, V3E 1P1
Phone: (604) 941-3041
Fax: (604) 944-7993

US Address
1300 Boblett Street
Unit A-218
Blaine, WA 98230
Phone: (866) 492-6623
Fax: (250) 493-6603

The price of success is hard work, dedication to the job at hand, and the determination that whether we win or lose, we have applied the best of ourselves to the task at hand.
Vince Lombardi

If you do not believe in working your field of opportunity, then this book is not for you. As Vince Lombardi so elegantly put it, success is hard work. There is no way around it. Someone has to do the work. Whether you are a great athlete, business professional or musician, achievement takes time, passion and effort. Accept it and embrace it; then you will be ready to embark on your journey of success.
Elton Pride

What Others Say About This Book

The title says, The Ultimate Small Business Owner's Guide, *however, the concepts can be applied to your business or personal life. This is a must read if you are looking to expand your business or make changes in your personal life. His stories are outstanding and full of insight, and his five steps will give you that competitive edge.*

Doug Carter, EQUIP—Senior Vice President

There is nothing more frustrating than knowing what you want to do and not knowing how to get it done. In The Ultimate Small Business Owner's Guide, *Elton Pride lays out a plan that can become your blueprint for success. Read the book, apply the steps and savor your successful outcome.*

Lisa Niemkiewicz, actress and professional facilitator

After reading The Ultimate Small Business Owner's Guide, *you will look at your business in a whole different light. This book outlines five simple steps business owners can take to increase their business. If your desired outcome is more customers and more money in less time, read the book and apply the steps. Elton Pride does a great job in laying out a plan that works—if you apply it. Elton shares his personal story, which is compelling and insightful. His book points readers in the right direction toward success. Study it and put the steps into action; they're simple and are sure to bring you great rewards.*

**Lisa Sasevich, The Queen of Sales Conversion &
#1 Best-Selling Author,** *The Live Sassy Formula*

After you read The Ultimate Small Business Owner's Guide, *you will look at both your business and daily success track from a different perspective and you will be glad you did.*

Don Staley, #1 Best-Selling Author, *Fit Mind, Fit Body*

Starting and operating a business is hard work; it's not for the faint of heart. Elton's book addresses the issue of dedication and hard work head on. This is a must-read for anyone thinking about starting a business and those of us who own a business. Read the book and get the truth about what it takes to get started and stay in business.

Howard Owen, business owner and entrepreneur

Contents

Acknowledgements

My life has been like having to figure out a puzzle and a combination lock all in one. I like to do things on my own. I'd rather be the Lone Ranger ("Hi Ho Silver") or the sole hero out ahead of the pack. However, over the years I've discovered the secret to putting the puzzle together and unlocking the combination lock has been *not* to go it alone. I've built relationships and received feedback from people I was close to and those I had kept at arm's length. I have worked hard and am responsible for my own success. However, as I've moved from puzzle to puzzle along my journey, all of my success has been because someone has *spoken* into my life.

Not empty words or hype, but words of advice and suggestions. I had to decide if I would listen or not, and when I listened it really paid off financially and in other ways as well. Family, friends, even foes advised, recommended and listened. After the conversations it was always completely up to me to respond to the suggestions and then decide my next move. I was determined to make the right choices and be successful.

I have been blessed to have so many people play a role in my development at different stages in my life. I won't attempt to name everyone. Instead, I'll say thank you to all the people who have contributed to my success.

Some individuals fall under what I call the elite category. These people helped to form my character, faith and core concepts. Without them, my foundation would have been built on shifting sands. My grandmother, Bessie Howard, raised me along with eight other children. Without a doubt, my grandmother was the most important person in my life as I grew up. She provided me with a great place to live and life lessons that still impact my life. She instilled in me the power of prayer, faith, education and hard work. The tough decisions she made for me when I was young laid the groundwork for my being able to share this book with you today. My grandmother introduced me to helper and leadership qualities at an early age. She truly blessed my life.

My mother, Mildred Howard, gave me the opportunity to be me; she gave me life and support growing up. When my mother came to visit, my grandmother would turn the reins back over to her. This gave my mother a chance to speak differently into my life. I got into trouble during one of those visits and my mother put me in a *timeout*. My grandmother didn't believe in *timeouts*. If you did something wrong you got a whipping on the spot. Case closed. I liked the *timeout* and remember thinking, "This is easy; I can do this all day." Still, it all worked out and I got the point. My aunts Ruth McCreary, Ruby Jackson, Lisa Hill, Bessie Gaillard and Velma Grimes, my grandmother's daughters, all took part in raising me, some more than others, like Bessie and Ruby.

My Aunt Bessie, still in the house during most of my upbringing, spent a lot of time nurturing me, so much people thought *she* was my mother. I remember when she went for her very first job interview for a human resources position with the Navy. My grandmother told her, "You will get the job. Go in with confidence and repeat the 23rd Psalms as you make your way to the interview." My aunt got the job. That led to my working summers with the military.

I sincerely appreciate everything this group of strong women imparted to me—communication skills, cooking, cleaning and good hygiene practices, just to name a few. With their input and that of my uncles, Lucas Thurman Howard (Buddy), Clarence

Jackson (Papa), Lonnie Grimes and Wilson Gaillard Jr. (Pete), I received everything I needed. I knew I was not a fifth wheel, even though I may have felt like I was imposing on them. I finally realized they all loved and cared for me, making sure I had everything I needed to succeed. Thank you for all the insight and love, which was added to my life.

Family and non-family members influenced me in my early years by helping me build foundations in what I call *my core outlets* -- running/track, guitar, photography, reading and sports. I am still active in all areas.

Running/Track—Uncle Buddy, Coach Richard Erwin, Coach Bill McClure, Coach Boots Garland

Guitar—Aunt Ruth (gave me my first guitar), Mr. Henry Grad (taught me guitar for seven years at no cost to me or my family)

Photography—Wayne Peacock (*exposed* me to photography), Aunt Bessie (helped me to purchase my first 35 mm camera), George Kings (while in the Navy, he served as President Eisenhower's photographer; taught me photography for three years at no cost to me or my family)

Reading—Captain Isaac (retired Navy Captain; tutor, taught me reading after my "OUCH" setback)

Sports—Ronald Townsend and family (took me and his sons, Ronnie and Matt, to my first college football game at the University of Florida and for my first time, to the Bayou Classic in New Orleans)

To my daughters, Sarah and Mary, I love you both more than you can ever imagine. I am always thinking of ways I can share with you so you will be all you have been called to be. I know at times you want to say, "Dad enough already." I hope you know it is all because I want the very best for you. True love works that way, always wanting to give the best. Never stop dreaming, never give up and always be willing to work to get what belongs to you. True love is also unconditional. May your prince in shining armor not be smoke and mirrors. Instead, may he be the true gift that God has waiting for you. Remember you deserve the best so be patient. As you move forward, what is yours will be revealed. All we have shared will never be forgotten. Whether memories captured through pictures or memories remembered, know I love you always unconditionally.

To my wife Edith, as of this writing it has been twenty-five years since we said "I Do." I can't say it has all been easy, because I would be lying, but I can say all the hard work has been worth it. We have navigated some ferocious waters together, all of which has made us stronger. It is through those times and others I have come to realize your true value as a friend, woman and wife. You are a beautiful, wise and strong woman who has had to deal with a lot of *stuff* throughout your life. I am amazed at your resilience, and how you continue to step up and be a gift to me. I honor you as a friend, woman and my wife; always know I love you and appreciate you for who you are.

Thank you to everyone past and many present at JM Family Enterprises—Southeast Toyota Distributors. I spent 20 years at this great company, learning from and with the very best in the industry. Specific thanks go to—Mark Miller, who cracked open the door of opportunity for me at JM Family. Mark signed up as my first joint venture partner with my first company, Soteria Design Technology, while he was working at ComputerLand. To Kathy Stried and Darryl Head, who took a chance on an entrepreneur looking to expand his knowledge in technology and business. To the innovative and generous Mr. Jim Moran.

Although Mr. Moran is no longer with us, I still think about him often, and about the environment he created that allowed me to learn the automotive business, increase my abilities and share my ideas. It was because of that opportunity I am able to operate the business I have today.

Finally, thank you to Nancy Gumina, who has been editing my work for the last fifteen years. Nancy provides writing and editing insight that casts a great reflection on me. Her work on this project has helped me show individuals and business owners how to discover, develop and fulfill their calling to reach more customers and increase their bottom line.

Preface

The "If Factor™"

If you do this you will get this result for you and your business.

You all have heard people say, *if I would have, I could have* (you fill in the blank).

Here are some examples:

o   If I had gone back to school, I would have my degree by now.

o   If I had invested my money wisely, I would have more money for retirement.

o   If I had been more frugal with my spending, I would have the money to start my own business.

o   If I had written a business plan, I would have a better idea of where I am going.

o   If I had joined a business mastermind group, I would be much further along with my business.

o   If I had been more consistent with my training program, I would be in better shape today.

As I share the following childhood story, please think about how you as an individual or business owner may have **missed opportunities** because **YOU chose not to step up, take action and make a difference**. If I would have I could have goes out the window when you give 100%. When you work at something 100% and you fail, that failure becomes a stepping-stone to your next challenge. If I would have disappears, because now you know for a fact it will not work. You will not waste time, energy or emotion wondering "what if." You can now move on to your next opportunity. As you read, be willing to step up and out of your comfort zone and into an unknown place—a place with results for you and your business. As you read, you will be rewarded with ideas on how to attract future customers and keep current customers happy, increasing what you need most—cash flow.

When I was 12 years old during one of Pensacola's humid summers, my friends and I were running in the back yard, playing *tag* and *army*. At the end of the day, I retreated to our back porch where my Uncle Buddy was repairing a mirror. My uncle called me over and said the following:

> *From the way you were playing out there, it looks like you could be a runner.* **If** *you would like to develop your running and get better at it, go out every day and run around the block five to six times and* **you will** *develop your running ability.*

The next day, I started a process that lasted for months. I would run around the block five to six times. My friends laughed at me—"Man, what are you doing, you look crazy." I responded, "My uncle said if I run around the block every day I can get good at it." I persisted and increased my running to one and two miles a day.

During those times, I did not have running shoes or a stop watch. I ran in my everyday tennis shoes—the same shoes I wore to school and around the house.

My stopwatch was my grandmother who kept track of my time. I alerted her when I left the house, and when I returned I yelled in the front window so she'd know I was back. She noted the time, making comments like, "It took you longer" or "You're getting better every day, keep it up."

"If" changed my life forever and started a process I will never forget. During my years at Pensacola Catholic High I was a C student, at best. As you know, that won't get you into college, not the ones I was interested in. By following through on my uncle's "If" challenge, I **discovered the running ability hidden in me**. Once discovered, I went on to develop my ability as an athlete. Doors previously closed were opened to me. Suddenly everything started to come together for me at Pensacola Catholic High—development, execution and the unveiling of my athletic talents to the world.

Because of the "If" challenge, I was able to generate over $130,000 in scholarships from high school, college and graduate school over an 11-year period. I earned a scholarship to a private high school, two state championships in the 330 intermediate hurdles and a full track scholarship to Louisiana State University (400 meters, 400 meter hurdlers and mile relay—indoor record held for 10 years). I received offers from the University of Florida, Auburn University, Florida State, Troy University and Furmen University (for football). After LSU, I was offered a full academic scholarship to graduate school at Rochester Institute of Technology (RIT).

The "If" challenge was a pathfinder for me. I received rejection letters because of my academic status, but I was able to attend the college of my choice because of my athletic ability. This all began with my Uncle Buddy's simple "If" challenge. However, I learned very quickly my athletic ability *got* me in, but it would not *keep* me in an environment of higher education. I would have to up my game. "If" I wanted to stay at LSU, I would have to learn the university education system and find my balance between education, college fun and athletics.

My educational journey had started taking some strange turns much earlier in life. I began my learning and athletic endeavors at a young age. I grew up in Pensacola, Florida, and attended LA Kersey Elementary School from first through third grades. I was promoted to fourth grade, but my very wise grandmother knew the real Elton. She realized I had not learned what a third grader should learn, like reading, and made a tough decision about the rest of my life. Even though all my friends were promoted to fourth grade, she held me back. Not to third grade. I went all the way back to second grade. (OUCH!) I was starting over, and at a different school, but it opened my eyes to a whole new world of opportunity. At St. Joseph I was made to learn, exposed to music (the guitar) and photography, and had the chance to expand my running ability.

I'm not on an ego trip here. I'm sharing this information to show you the power of the "If" factor and the impact other people can have on your life. Many people contributed to my success. My mother, Mildred, made it possible for me to be me. My grandmother Bessie raised me, kept track of my time (and not just while running) and gave me my moral compass. You already know all about the importance of my Uncle Buddy's "If" challenge. My Aunts Bessie, Ruby, Ruth and Velma took care of me and made sure I did all the right things. My Uncle Clarence gave me insight into family life dynamics in a personally meaningful way, allowing me to build a picture in my mind I would one day apply to my own family. Along life's journey there were many athletic coaches, mentors and friends' fathers who included me in their family activities and *just for the guys* athletic events.

In reflecting on my life experiences, what Steve Jobs called "connecting the dots,"[1] I've learned there is a monetary value associated with everything you do and don't do. It will either cost you time or money. We have all heard time is money. "If" you want to save yourself time and money, you have to step up and listen to the little things others may be saying around you. Consider how you can use those insights (positive or negative) to your advantage. The bottom line is you have to filter feedback, keeping what will propel you in a positive direction and releasing what may hinder your path and hold you back. I call it a **selection filter**. After the selection is made, place all useful information in your **backpack of life** for present or future use. It is all about the choices you make that will hinder you, enhance you monetarily or benefit you in some other form. For me it all started from my uncle's "If" challenge: "**If** you would like to develop your running and get better at it, go out every day and run around the block five to six times and **you will** develop your running ability."

What about you? If you had done something differently, would you have more positive results today? Are you getting all the results you've always dreamed about as an individual or business owner? Are you:

o   Creating the cash you need?

o   Getting the promotions you think you've earned?

o   Building the relationships you want?

o   Writing the business plan you need?

o   Starting or expanding your business?

o   Going back to school? Earning that degree?

o   Fulfilling other life-long dreams?

If you follow the concepts in this book, you can achieve great results and reap your rewards. I invite you to go on a journey of learning and self-discovery. I designed this book to help you make changes in your life that will affect you and the operation of your business. The book contains many of my life lessons and secrets learned along the way. I've also included excerpts from some of my best newsletters. I'm sharing them with you to encourage, motivate and inspire you to take action. However, you will get nothing other than my thoughts and ideas just from reading the pages. If you are looking for real change—enrichment in your relationships, business or income, you have to get up and make it happen. Bottom line—you have to do it. Not your mother, father, sister, brother, cousin, friend, boss … YOU.

If you ACT, you will enter a new phase in your life and you will never be the same. You will ignite your imagination as you move through the pages of this book. Here's your first action step—complete the book and **as you get to the end I'll give you the opportunity to determine your next big move for you and your business**.

Far better is it to dare mighty things, to win glorious triumphs, even though checked by failure … than to rank with those poor souls who neither enjoy much nor suffer much, because they live in a gray twilight that knows not victory nor defeat.
Theodore Roosevelt[2]

There is a price to pay for gaining success in your world and the world around you. Are you ready to step up and make things happen for YOU? If so, turn the page.

Elton Pride

The PRIDE™ 5-Step Process

Here is an overview of the process that has brought me increased income, great gains and personal rewards—The **PRIDE™** 5-Step Process. It's easy to use "If" you follow it. Each chapter will walk you through one step, providing ample examples and explanation. As you move through the steps, apply the information to your own life and business. I hope it brings you as much success, prosperity and happiness as it has brought me.

PRIDE™ 5-Step Process

Step 1 - *Purpose and Passion:*
You and Your Business Must Exist for a Purpose

Step 2 - *Right Choices:*
The Choices You Make Matter

Step 3 - *Infinite Insight:*
Believe in Yourself and Your Business

Step 4 - *Discover Your Opportunities:*
Take Advantage of the Good and the Bad

Step 5 - *Execute Your Plan:*
MOVE—Make Things Happen—Work Your Plan

Chapter 1
You and Your Business Must
Exist for a Purpose

*If you don't know where you're going, any road
will take you there.*
Lewis Carroll
Paraphrased from Alice in Wonderland[3]

Thousands of books have been written on the subject and importance of finding one's purpose in life. A recent Mercer survey of 30,000 workers in 17 worldwide locations showed between 28% and 56% of employees wanted to leave their jobs. In the U.S., 32% said they wanted to find new work.[4]

Why are so many people unhappy with their present jobs, and why don't they do something about it? Everywhere you look there are free resources to help individuals find new jobs. Some might be reluctant to leave a job today, any job, when the economy is not in full recovery. Others may have looked, but no jobs were to be found. In either case, we all know people who are truly miserable in their jobs, just in it for the paycheck, not using their talents, unable to find a job or have given up on finding their purpose in life, if they ever looked for it. Maybe I'm describing you.

Purpose or Calling—Share Your Blessing

Purpose or *calling* in life? Wasn't there a high school counselor who said something to you about that once? Was it really *that* long ago when you last gave any thought to purpose or *calling*—a strong conviction toward a vocation, profession or vision to do something meaningful in life?

Everyone has an assignment or calling. You're not here just to consume air, water and food, crossing off the days on a calendar. Each of you has something unique, a *blessing* you can share with others in words or actions. As an individual or a business, you bless others through your calling with something they need, desire or want. Sometimes they are clueless about what you have to offer.

Your **blessing** is a **special gift or talent** you're good at, such as selling, organizing, painting, speaking or writing. When you share your gift, you are blessing someone who needs it and it becomes a blessing in their life. Your unique ability can often bring **monetary value** to your life if you pursue, develop and use it appropriately.

You have opportunities to both give and receive blessings. Here's the tricky part. When on the receiving end, you must recognize when someone is attempting to bless you. Somebody in passing says, "Hey, you may want to try this idea in your business." You could choose not to listen or listen but call it a dumb idea. Instead, you could identify it as a blessing and choose to thoughtfully consider it and do it. The idea could potentially save or make you money. You'll never know unless you are open to seeing it as a potential opportunity. The final decision to use the information is always up to you.

I've been talking about purpose, calling and blessing. You may also have heard these names—sweet-spot, your voice, genius, reason for living and so on. It doesn't matter what you call it. In fact, I gave it a name with special meaning for me:

C alling

A ssignment

L iving in

M e

I have used my CALM™ to help myself and others; others have used their CALM™ to help me when I requested help, and I'm sure, when I was clueless about needing help. From here on in, I'll use CALM™ and the words **purpose** and **calling** interchangeably, as **they mean the same thing. Your** CALM™ **will play a large role in your overall individual and business success**.

Many people ignore their CALM™ because it takes work, effort and persistence. Would you rather work on a business plan *or* play computer Solitaire while sipping a Latte Grande? Your CALM™ will not magically drop from the sky. You have to discover, develop and execute your CALM™. You have all the tools you need. All the concepts, opportunities and innovation you need to accomplish this are available for the taking—if—you are looking for them. Others may share their insights. I had a *eureka* moment when my uncle gave me his "If" challenge. I could have brushed off his comments and missed all I've gained by confirming his insight. You need to be in a place of:

- o   Heightened awareness
- o   Receptivity
- o   Readiness to confirm or deny others' insights

to capitalize on these potential *eureka* moments. As you reveal the calming effect in your life, your CALM™, you are now on the road to catching up to where your heart already is. More about this later.

What if some stranger came up to you on the street and said, "Do this one thing and many of your issues in life will be resolved," would you stop to listen? Would you do that one thing? Would you be surprised to learn the one thing *universally important* to all individuals is to—

Determine Your Life's Purpose

Now I'm transitioning into more of a clarification and application section on purpose and calling. This will help you to apply the concepts to your life.

Remember, I said purpose is the same as one's CALM™.

So we're all on the same page, Webster's Dictionary says,

> ***Purpose*** is: *1. the reason for which something exists or is done, made, or used, 2. an intended or desired result; end aim; goal, 3. determination; resoluteness.*[5]

Is Your Life Defined by Purpose?

Purpose helps to define why we exist, and it provides three essential elements in our lives: *focus*, *intent* and *discipline*.

When people think of **discipline** they tend to think of self-control. "Don't even think about eating that chocolate donut or hot glazed Krispy Kreme." There's more to discipline than depriving you of chocolate and hot donuts. Discipline supplies inner strength to reach goals despite distractions and setbacks.

It builds personal power, leading to higher self-confidence and self-esteem. Discipline is the medicine most of us would rather do without. However, it is essential in the healing of our wants and achieving success.

Purpose introduces *focus* and *intent* to your life. **Focus** is the ability to hone in on what is most important, no matter how loud the noise and clutter around you. In the world of photography, focus is defined in four ways: In-focus, out-of-focus, soft-focus or sharp-focus. The idea is you must lead the viewer through the picture by using the focus method. The eye must be led to the main focus of the picture, otherwise the viewer will just wander through the picture; much like individuals wander through life with no focus. Sometimes focus is simply saying *"No."*

Live your life with **intent**, pursuing what you have been called to do. Journey toward something that fits; acknowledge you have a life of purpose and grant it the right to live and exist. What are your intentions? What could you hope to get out of the actions you are about to take or not take? Intent is a noun that requires action. Your intention brings together focus and discipline which creates results.

Empowerment through Purpose

Purpose adds invigorating personal energy, creativity, ingenuity and sense of self-worth to your life. When you move through life *without* **purpose**, you give away your power and fail to realize your original *intent* for existing. Every action and thought should be focused on creating your best self. Empowerment comes from removing instability and becoming what lives in the core of your being—by finding the calling living in you; by finding and developing your special gifts. Become the person you were meant to be. Find your **purpose** in life.

I found purpose at a very young age thanks to my Uncle Buddy. He noticed my running potential and planted a thought in me—I could develop my running ability by working on my running skills. I had focus, intent and discipline which led to my eventual success. I didn't just wake up one day and start winning races. I had to go through a process of development. I learned how to be disciplined, work hard and smart, learn from others and give to others what I had learned. I had no idea where I would end up—I kept moving forward to a positive rhythm, adjusting my course as I filtered feedback along the way.

Running had become a way out for me, and every step forward cleared the path for other opportunities. Each step also had a value in time and money. Like you, I had to choose how to invest my time and take advantage of what I had before me. As I grew, my running ability greatly improved. Running became a portal of opportunity to express myself in a way I never had before. I was in my place, **my place of purpose**. I was moving with intent, **investing in me**.

Place of Purpose

*An established **vision** is like a river; it will go over, around and under anything to get to the **place of purpose** that has been set and focused in the mind.*

Elton Pride

Once you have a **vision** of where you are going in life or business, every learning, misstep and even opposition can be used as a stepping-stone to your next victory. When you are *not* in your **place of purpose** (wrong job, wrong career, with the wrong person, etc.), you should be **preparing for your place of purpose by learning all you can where you are**.

A young lady I'll call Tracy is a successful entrepreneur and owner of her dream business—a funeral home. I'll have to go back 15 years to show *how* **she arrived at her place of purpose**.

Tracy may have made her calling breakthrough by reading, watching the Discovery Channel, attending a funeral or someone's suggestion. She realized early on she loved mortuary science. While in high school, Tracy spent several days a week being mentored at a local funeral home. She learned the importance of community involvement, dealing with people in emotional times, burial preparation and the entire business operation. These actions moved her closer to her eventual goal of one day owning her own funeral business.

Recognizing her zeal, passion and purpose-driven life, I wanted to invest in her dream early. I gave her a gift of $100 for her high school graduation with this instruction: "This is the beginning of your seed money to start your business. Invest it and save it for that purpose." I have no idea if she followed my advice, but I do know she earned her mortuary science degree, learned the business by working for others and started her dream business.

Tracy's success didn't happen by accident. Her thoughtful and deliberate actions (intent) over time turned thought into reality— she made the right choices, invested time, put in the work, secured opportunities and sought help as needed. She was on a mission with *vision, passion* and *insight*. When that happens the universe lines things up in your favor. In Tracy's case, planners, workers and investors came forward *wanting* to help her.

I recently heard a TV producer explain what television really is—tell-a-vision. Individuals paying for the ad or program are telling you their vision. Tracy shared her vision and investors emerged to support her. Select the appropriate time to tell your vision and you may be amazed at the support you will receive.

Walt Disney put it this way, "You can design and create, and build the most wonderful place in the world. But it takes people to make the dream a reality."[6] However it happens for you, with ease or a long, drawn-out discovery process, finding your *place* is vital to your overall success. Perseverance and determination will get you there.

Learning Where You Are ...
When You Don't Like Where You Are

Where you are at the moment may not be a comfortable or happy place for you, but **make it a place of learning**. Use your time there to prepare yourself for your eventual *place of purpose*—I call that **learning where you are**. It makes *where you are* more tolerable and better positions you for your eventual *place of purpose*.

I'll share how I came up with this concept. When I was in high school a group of friends and I skipped class and went to the beach. Needless to say, we got into big trouble. Before the hammer dropped on us my teacher said, "I hope you enjoyed **every moment** of your escapade, because I assure you, **you will be present** here and won't enjoy your punishment."

As I built my career in corporate America, I always remembered and applied the **"you will be present"** talk. My burning desire was to start my own company. It required being present in the moment with everything I did, including my involvement in five start-ups and spending 20 years with a dynamic company. I have followed my teacher's wise words—**you will be present**—in every job. I have purposefully:

✓ Worked on my attitude of being completely present
✓ Gathered insight from everyone around me

✓ Fine-tuned my skills
✓ Developed new skills
✓ Dressed for the role at hand and the one in the crosshairs

If I was going to spend any of my day's 86,400 seconds in a place of "insight," I had better get something out of it to prepare to start my own company. I made each job a learning experience for the next job. Along the way, I started a company—learning what it means to be on your own, the importance of a business plan and cash flow, the ups and downs of having partners and rising and falling while making mistakes. I returned to the corporate world, but I knew in my heart I would start my own company again someday.

During my hiatus from small business I remained *in the moment,* **using the time to enhance skills and expand my network**. I stayed on course toward my ultimate place of purpose and doing what I love—being an entrepreneur. I had detours and bumps along the way. However, I had a vision and a plan to get there; knowing this kept me moving in the right direction.

<u>**Remember, learn where you are now, even if you hate it, even if it's painful; it is *not* a waste of time.**</u> If you're in a class you hate or a dead-end job with a horrible boss, you can learn how *not* to manage others, how *not* to lead, how *not* to communicate or how *not* to delegate. **All of this is learning**; you will be able to use it at another time and in another place. Look up, get up and continue moving in the direction of your desire outcome.

Economy Got You Feeling *Skittish*?

I talked earlier about why people stay in their jobs if they're unhappy. People are in a place that pays the bills and they're skittish about jumping ship. In their hearts they know they should be someplace else.

Most people live in a very restricted circle of their potential being. We all have reservoirs of energy and genius to draw upon of which we do not dream.

William James[7]

If you're feeling a bit *skittish*, ask yourself these questions:

1. Why am I here?
2. What should I be learning to equip myself for the next place I would like to go?
3. How may I be sabotaging myself by not being open to those around me who may have the answers I need?

Use your time to enhance strategic skills and abilities. Include the areas that follow.

Enhance Your Knowledge in:

✓ Business dynamics
✓ Communication skills
✓ Leadership skills
✓ Building relationships
✓ Finance and Economics
✓ Entrepreneurship
✓ Learning unique to your industry and profession

Bridge Figure

Gain insights to help you **build your bridge from *where you are* to *where you are going*.** You are responsible for designing, orchestrating and implementing your plan to close this gap.

It's your future. You must be your own **bridge figure**, with strong touch points as you build and travel across the bridge to your planned outcome. **Touch points** serve as bridge beams, buttressing special attention areas in your plan. **Mastermind groups**, **coaches**, **mentors** or **friends** help with focus, obstacles and execution. As a business owner, one person is responsible for the success of your business: YOU. Therefore, **you accepting your role as a *bridge* figure is essential to the overall *health and profits* made in your company.**

Do You Know Where YOU Are Going?

It is very difficult to know where you are going when you can't see a picture of your final destination. It's like trying to assemble a 1000-piece puzzle without looking at the picture on the front of the box. However, to assemble it you must look at the picture and *work with the pieces provided.*

When it comes to your purpose you must also ***work with what you've got***. This could affect the possibilities you should be exploring. It may sound silly but you need to ***know what you've got***. Take personal inventory through reflection and self-discovery, both of which are impacted by *the way you think.*

It's All in Your Mind

Any thinking preventing you from seeing the real you impedes your progress. Your thoughts and the way you see yourself *must* change if you plan to excel, going where only you can go as an individual or in business. In his book *As a Man Thinketh*, James Allen recognized the impact of thought as follows:

All that a man achieves and all that he fails to achieve is the direct result of his own thoughts. As he thinks, so he is; as he continues to think, so he remains.[8]

It all starts in the mind, so it's essential you **think of yourself from a perspective of greatness**. Every thought you allow to bed in your mind takes root and grows, producing good or bad thoughts that will create opportunity or opposition. The decision is yours. Thought is alive and in most cases manifests itself through ideas and imagination.

Your vision is one of your keys of success. All things are created three times: first, as **thoughts**; second, as a **plan**; third, as a **physical creation**. I am talking about a process of re-creating you. Your purpose represents your desires, dreams, hopes, goals, plans and aspirations. Take heart in what you are embarking on and involve your entire being. When body, mind and spirit are completely engaged, you will prevail. However, when you are not totally committed to an outcome, you will have twice the opposition—your internal conflict *and* all the things life will throw at you. Review the 4-Step Pyramid Process that follows for more details.

4-Step Pyramid Process

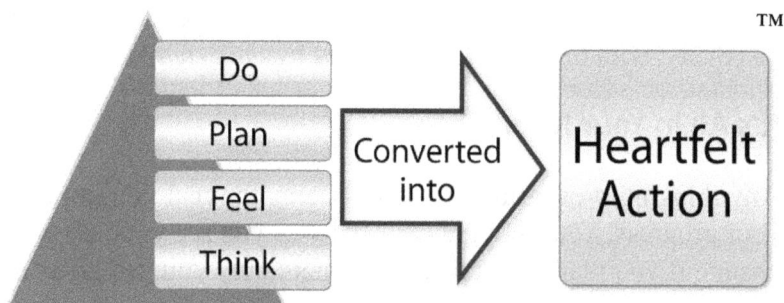

TM

Do
Plan
Feel
Think

Converted into

Heartfelt Action

1. **Think:** Good or bad thoughts create progress or opposition. The decision is yours.
2. **Feel:** Feelings are created from being what you expect to become. Be it now.

3. **Plan:** How will you get there? Create your road map.

4. **Do:** Finally some type of action occurs—Good, Bad or Indifferent. Once executed, your thought becomes heartfelt action.

Watch your thoughts; they become words. Watch your words; they become actions. Watch your actions; they become habit. Watch your habits; they become character. Watch your character; it becomes your destiny.

Lao Tzu[9]

Are You Getting Started?

Find the purpose living in you. It may bring you *more* opposition because life is full of challenges. Don't let that deter you. You can **take charge of your life by simply getting started**. Begin moving in a direction to fuel your inner calling and get closer to your desired goal.

Have you ever heard of "The Ripple Effect"? No, it's not the effect of drinking too much of *Fred Sanford's*[10] favorite wine. If you throw a pebble in a pond, the water ripples fan out from where the stone hit the water. This triggers a domino effect of activities—fish jumping, ducks quacking, birds flying away, and so on. All these events occur from your one simple action. The same applies to you and the ripple effect your actions have. By doing what you love and being good at it, you might help others start their journey. When will your pebble go in the water?

Hidden in Plain Sight

Finding your purpose is a journey requiring planning, collaboration, hard work and commitment to leverage the experience. As you develop your purpose, you will continue to share your blessing with others, as an individual or through your business. Take purpose seriously and milk it for all you can. Know that your purpose belongs to you and it's up to you to find it. You may find this hard to believe, but **your purpose is probably hidden in plain sight**. Ask yourself this question:

What do I always end up talking about or doing that helps others?

Your response will get you closer to discovering your CALM™.

It's Your Move

Many great authors, Jack Canfield, John Maxwell, Myles Munroe and others, have written books about *purpose*. I encourage you to read their work for more insight.

If you are satisfied with where you are, then there is no need to read any further. However, if you feel **there is more for you in life**, if you would **be excited to have a life with passion**, keep reading.

A Life with Passion

If your mind is in the boudoir, I'm not talking about *that* kind of passion. *A Life with Passion* refers to the passion for life and work within you, your CALM™.

Search inward to find the unique gifts and talents that excite; be willing to develop and share them with the world, releasing the potential within, creating success as an individual and small business owner.

Purpose–Passion Connection

Passion is closely aligned with purpose. How many people have you met who said they'd work for free? They love what they do so much, they can't believe they get paid for it. Steve Jobs was one of those people. To the very end, Jobs was **driven by passion**—for his company, innovation and doing things right. Jobs said, "Great products only come from people who are passionate ... You have to be burning with an idea, or a problem, or a wrong that you want to right."[11]

The World English Dictionary says,

> **Passion** is: *the object of an intense desire, ardent affection, or enthusiasm.*[12]

When Jobs described what he hoped his legacy would be, he began with the word *passion*—"My passion has been to build an enduring company where people were motivated to make great products."[13] What are you passionate about? Do you enjoy what you are doing so much you'd be willing to do it just for the JOY of IT? Is what you are doing in your life now the result of choices you made or choices you allowed someone else to make for you? It is easier to be successful when you are driven by passion which is shaped by discipline and fuelled with focus and intent. Passion is required when opposition seeks to undermine your efforts. Your passion will help you to face adversity and say, "I'm still alive and ready to continue my journey."

The prime rule of reality is that we must become in our lives what we choose to experience in the world.
Gregg Braden[14]

Do You "Get It"?

No matter how much you plan, emergencies happen and you must drop everything and deal with the situation. Recently, I had to call timeout and deal with a death in my family. I was reminded of a quote from Steve Jobs:

Remembering that I'll be dead soon is the most important tool I've ever encountered to help me make the big choices in life. Because almost everything—all external expectations, all pride, all fear of embarrassment or failure—these things just fall away in the face of death, leaving only what is truly important ... There is no reason not to follow your heart.[15]

For Jobs, mortality brought an intensified **clarity of *purpose* and *passion* to his life**. He really "got it." Do you need to face death to reach the same intensity and clarity to follow your passion and your heart—to "get it?"

The reality is time is short for all of us. Everything you dreamed of and hoped for might never happen because you hesitated out of fear, laziness or lack of money. If you had the chance to change your fate and it required hard work, discipline and reaching out to others, would you be willing to make all the sacrifices necessary? How you answer this question can determine if YOU "Get It." To "be it" and "get it" you may have to end something and start something new, revealing sacrifice and hard work, but also higher levels of success for you.

Life does not last forever, so do what you are passionate about, what drives you, if it:

- Involves integrity
- Is aligned with your core beliefs
- Will change your life for the better

Don't wait; you should be doing it ***RIGHT NOW!***

When you catch up with your heart you "Get It."
It's then that your passion takes on a laser focus,
driving you toward success.
Elton Pride

What Are You Becoming?

Every Olympic athlete had to become a great athlete by practicing the results he or she wanted to obtain. Are you becoming what you choose to experience? Are you practicing and following your PASSION? Follow these tips:

1. Have the courage to be who you were created to be.
2. Invest the time to make the right things happen.
3. If you want something badly enough, you must be willing to work hard at it.
4. Recruit people to help you.
5. Make sacrifices which put you closer to your desired outcomes.
6. Be disciplined in your focus.
7. Know why you are doing it.

> *Lazy people want much but get little, but those who work hard will prosper and be satisfied.*
> *The Bible: Proverbs 13:4*[16]

If you want something you must work for it—

From the inside out,
From the heart up, to your head,
From the head out, to your action makers,
your arms and legs.

I was recently in Washington, D.C., and met **Carl Lewis**, widely believed to be one of the greatest athletes of all time. Lewis won nine gold medals from the 1984, 1988, 1992 and 1996 Olympic Games. Today he owns several thriving businesses. His success was not by chance. **He put his heart and soul into his dreams**

to be the best at his craft and millions saw the results of his hard work. Lewis continues to reap the benefits today from his intense training for the Olympics. By developing his running ability and performing at a high level of victory, today he is still able to build on that foundation to **produce great outcome in business**.

There is a financial payoff in doing what you love *if* you are excellent at your craft. Work your craft—study, practice, learn and relearn. **Apply all the tools at your disposal.** *If* you are excellent, then people will pay you to share your blessing—your CALM™. Be it. Be excellent at it and **get paid for it**. It works.

It's the same process for you as an individual and business owner. You don't have to be an Olympic gold medalist; however, you must work hard and smart, refine your craft and keep moving forward. **One day you will reap the long-term benefits of your commitment,** just like Carl Lewis, Steve Jobs or my neighbor Howard Owen, owner of Owen Business Systems. I have no doubt they would all agree on this; even when you love what you do, it still takes **passion, sacrifice, work, time and money to make your business succeed**.

Despite that, YOU have everything you need to change you and your business. I'll end this chapter with a story about how you have the tools at hand; even the simplest tools can have the biggest impact on your success.

It is through a PASSION for something that truth is revealed: Are you willing to do whatever it takes—sacrifice, fight for it, and "dig through the dung" if necessary? It is in those moments when you will discover your truth. It always comes back to **being present and willing to work through "stuff" to find *your gold* and process it**.

Chase down your passion like it's the last bus of the night.
Terri Guillemets[17]

Here I am with Gold Medal Winner Carl Lewis

I promised you a story about **simple tools to impact your success**. The following process can change you forever "if" you apply it. My grandmother was a woman who believed in prayer. She also believed in execution and work; these two things gave her prayers a chance to live. My grandmother got up early every day, knelt by her rocking chair and prayed. I watched her kneeling and later sitting in her rocking chair, writing down what appeared to be instructions. Later I'd see an empty chair, as my grandmother was now implementing her insight, downloaded from her universal source of life.

This rocking chair process showed me:

o   You get up to get down (you get out of bed to get down on your knees).

o   You get down to get up (from your knees you look up to get answers).

o   Then you MOVE to implement (you get up and make things happen).

As a business owner, want-to-be business owner or individual, you can benefit from tapping into what I call the *universal source*. Simply start the conversation and it will work for you. Read the *Rocking Chair Process* that follows.

Rocking Chair Process

1. Offer up thanks and ask for insight; be specific.
2. Write down the instructions you receive.
3. Say thanks; get up and execute.
4. See the results of your work.

Be opportunistic. If you are looking for the *universal source* to work on your behalf, you must be alert and open to all the *free* tangible and intangible tools available to you. Speak, ask, listen and reflect. Get out your rocking chair and make things happen by creating a great return on investment for your business.

Passion, **purpose** and **vision** are the vehicles to make you a generation-changer in your world. Find something you are truly passionate about and pursue it, be it, and uncover the unseen world of the new you in your business and personal life. Catch up with your heart and create positive change in your life, living through your CALM™.

Chapter 1—Points to Remember

1. Empower yourself by finding your unique calling, CALM™ or purpose in life.
2. Have the courage to be yourself and do what you love.
3. Expect to work hard and sacrifice.
4. Purpose and passion executed in the right way have a financial payoff.
5. Learn all you can where you are.

Ready to Take Action?

Experience the joy CALM™ brings

Make this transformation now!

Go to www.prideglobalmgmt.com/5secretsdownload1now

To download a form on: Discovering your CALM™

Chapter 2
The Choices You Make Matter

Life is a sum of all your choices.
Albert Camus[18]

Challenging Times

We live in challenging times. Working to increase income, start a business, keep or expand a business, find or keep a job—these are tough assignments in today's environment. It would be easy to get discouraged and give up. You have no control over gas prices, what the Fed Chairman will do with interest rates or even the weather; or do you?

Controlling Your Environment

When cold sets in, you put on a sweater or turn up the heat; if heat waves arrive, you sip a cold drink or turn on the air conditioning. In each of these situations, YOU are creating your environment of comfort by taking action to change YOU or your physical environment. You can do the same thing with your economic environment. Regardless of your situation and what's happening around you, **you can choose to create a world that rewards and sustains you**.

Positive Attitudes, Positive Choices

The choices you make matter. You always have **control over your attitude** and the choices you make. Why not choose an **attitude of success** and make choices to help move you forward? If you get turned down for a position, dust yourself off and go for another job. When one marketing promotion doesn't bring in as many customers as you had hoped, think of another way to increase business. Focus on how you can make it better. Ask yourself:

o   Why am I doing this?

o   Where did I make mistakes?

o   What mistakes did I make?

o   How can I do it better and differently?

o   Who can help me do it better and differently?

Reinforce this powerful focus by **being true to yourself** while **purposefully networking** with others who share the same sense of self and action orientation.

Ed Rensi, former McDonald's President and CEO, put it this way, "Do not stand by and let the rest of the world dictate how you're going to live your life. It's no fun living that way."[19]

Create an "Economy of Success" in *Any* Economy

YOU are completely responsible for creating the economy that will allow YOU to sustain YOU. It is just as easy to create a personal *economy of success* as it is to create an economy of failure; both require you to act. I work with clients across the country and they consistently grumble about the state of our present economy. The reality is there are issues with the economy. However, you must figure out how to take advantage of such a market—opportunity always lurks in opposition. I'll talk more about that later.

If you believe your business does not have a chance in hell in this economy, guess what, if you believe it, you are right. As we discussed in Chapter 1, when you work as a *bridge figure* you see the opposition *but* you still build the bridge of opportunity to your place of desired outcome.

Conscious Choices – Real Consequences

Consider this. Everything is monetized in some form. Whether you live in India or Trump Tower on Fifth Avenue in Manhattan, you get the same amount of time. The rubber meets the road when you make decisions and **choose** how you will use your time. Will you squander your time with what you are doing? You may *choose* to sleep away your hours, veg out on social media or use the same non-working tactics time after time in your business.

Realize those are **conscious choices** with real consequences to you and your business. Your choices may be losing you money because you could have been doing something else with your time, such as:

o   Developing a business plan to expand your business.

o   Making phone calls to generate new leads.

o   Conducting computer research on university business management programs to expand your knowledge.

Recognize everything you do has a value to it.

Trust Your Choices

In 2005, Steve Jobs delivered an inspirational commencement speech ("Stay Hungry, Stay Foolish") at Stanford University. He told a story called "connecting the dots" about a college calligraphy course he had taken with no practical application for him at the time. Years later it had a huge impact when they designed the first Mac computer with its beautiful typography. He could never have predicted it would play such a crucial role in his career and to the personal computer.

> *Of course it was impossible to connect the dots looking forward when I was in college. But it was very, very clear looking backwards ten years later ... So you have to trust that the dots will somehow connect in your future.*
> *Steve Jobs*[20]

Trust your choices. Believe you are making the best possible choices based on the information you have at hand. Don't second guess yourself.

Expect *Your* Dots to Connect

As I think about how I've gotten to where I am today, I look back at how my dots have connected. One of these "dot" experiences was especially important to my career. I was working as a computer software trainer in a large organization. A Vice President sat in the front row of one of my training sessions. Afterwards the VP complimented my performance.

Several years went by. I was in another job about to be phased out, and frankly, I was wondering where I was going next. Out of the blue, I received a phone call asking if I would like to interview for a position in the same region I had given the training session three years earlier. The position would report to the VP who had attended my session. I interviewed and got the job. In the interview the VP told me I had conducted a presentation three years ago and he wrote something down on a piece of paper that day. He showed me the paper and it said: "Elton is a guy I want to have work for my department whenever I have an opening." The dots connected. One session led to a promotion three years later.

A few lessons learned include:

o   How you conduct yourself when communicating, giving presentations, etc., is important and can leave a lasting impression.
o   You never know when senior executives or others will be searching for talent.

As a business owner you should always be on the lookout for outstanding talent; in most cases you will find it outside your industry. I also realized I had been following Dale Carnegie's principles. His simple and effective advice still rings true today.

Dale Carnegie's *Golden Book* stressed:

o   Always remember to give honest and sincere appreciation.
o   Be genuinely interested in other people.
o   Remember to smile.[21]

You may think these are very basic concepts but ask yourself, *"If I follow them consistently would they make a difference?"* They apply to employees and customers alike. You must use them with your employees if you expect your employees to use them with your customers.

Choose Positive Lasting Impressions

As I thought about my experience with the VP, I realized I had learned the lesson about making lasting impressions as a youth. I had four chores on Saturdays—clean my room, clean the bathroom, put out the trash and rake the yard. My grandmother taught me how to rake the yard, believe it or not, with a handmade rake made from tree branches. Eventually we got a store-bought rake and I became an expert. Neighbors saw my work and started asking who raked our yard. People began requesting me to rake their yards, at a fee of course.

Based on that experience, I learned you must always put your best foot forward because you never know *who will be watching or asking who did that work.*

This is critical in business. Potential new customers in the market for a new product or service provider could be observing your business, or listening to what your customers are saying about their experiences with your business. Observations (and word of mouth) can make lasting impressions to help or hinder your business. The quality of your work matters and speaks to your craft, even if the craft is raking leaves. Martin Luther King, Jr. said it this way:

> *If a man is called to be a street sweeper, he should sweep streets even as Michelangelo painted, or Beethoven composed music, or Shakespeare wrote poetry. He should sweep streets so well all the host of heaven and earth will pause to say, here lived a great street sweeper who did his job well.*[22]

My yard raking business lessons went even deeper. My grandmother was teaching me five things: the importance of visibility, trust, innovation, increase and work.

1. **Visibility** – What your yard looks like matters. If you faithfully care for your yard's *appearance*, it will position you to receive more; you've shown you are more likely to care for a larger yard.

2. **Trust** – My grandmother recognized I had learned the yard-raking job well; she *believed in me* and *trusted* the task would be done weekly, so she turned it over to me.

3. **Innovation** – Making a rake from tree branches was a *creative* way of using what you have to produce what you need. Innovative thinking leads to a mind open to opportunity which will serve you well.

4. **Increase** – When you take care of what belongs to you, respect its purpose (use), and strive to be your best, you will acquire monetary *rewards*.

5. **Work** – Someone has to put the time in to create results of a yard well done.

Life lessons are preludes to business ingenuity. It is your responsibility to thread together the garment that fits your desired outcome.
Elton Pride

Making the *Right* Decisions

To get somewhere you must be moving. As you move, you must make choices about direction, people you will surround yourself with and decisions you will make about your career and business.

Every decision you make will *not* be the right decision and that's fine. **What's most important is that you make a decision**, right or wrong, and let the chips fall where they may. I'm not talking about thoughtless decisions. I'm referring to decisions based on sound information, input from others and true gut insights. This will allow you to keep moving in an informed way.

Your automatic guidance system cannot guide you when you're standing still.
Maxwell Maltz[23]

Fear often prevents people from making the right choices or making any choices. Fear of failure, success, being wrong, embarrassed by what others will say. Have I mentioned your fear? Consider the fear of having *someone else* make the choices for YOUR LIFE or BUSINESS. The choices you make matter so much; they affect your wealth, health and joy and yet you hesitate to make crucial decisions about your own life. Now that is real fear. Who better than you to make decisions that will affect the big 3 – YOUR wealth, YOUR health and YOUR overall joy in life?

No matter what choice you make there will be some struggle, apprehension and discomfort. Identify when and what kind of advice you need to succeed and surround yourself with individuals who can help you. Don't expect to have competencies in every area yourself. Tap into your contacts: mastermind group, mentor, friends and your *universal source*. Choose to stay focused on your end goal and never give up. Base your decisions on your life's guiding values and core principles. Do you know what yours are? If not, this would be a great time to put your list of guiding values in writing. Take a moment and consider yours.

Will you take action by throwing the pebble in the water, or will you stand there and think about it? Make a choice to change you and your business for the better. Choose to turn your thoughts into action, because it all matters.

Consult not your fears but your hopes and dreams. Think not about your frustrations, but about your unfulfilled potential. Concern yourself not with what you tried and failed in, but with what is still possible for you to do.
Pope John XXIII[24]

Chapter 2—Points to Remember

1. You have more control than you think.
2. You can control your attitude and your choices.
3. Choose an attitude of success.
4. Trust your choices; make a decision.
5. Make positive lasting impressions with current and potential customers.
6. Seek out advice, but don't leave it to others to make decisions for you.
7. Everything you do matters and affects the outcome.

Ready to Take Action?

Live a life of right choices.

Make this transformation now!

Go to www.prideglobalmgmt.com/5secretsdownload2now

To download a form on: Making Right Choices

Chapter 3
Believe in Yourself and Your Business

Know Yourself

Frederick the Great of Prussia was walking in Berlin when he met an old man. "Who are you?" asked Frederick. "I am a king," replied the old man. "A king!" laughed Frederick. "Over what kingdom do you reign?" "Over myself," the man proudly replied.[25]

You need to know your values, weaknesses and strengths to operate your business effectively. Self-awareness makes true self-expression, acceptance and change possible. Broaden your strengths and devise a plan to improve weaknesses. Surround yourself with people who are smarter than you. You may struggle with the idea at first. Having the right people in your circle will fill in your weak areas and those you have no time to address. This is what successful business people do. They also take personal inventory. Ask someone you trust, who will be totally honest, these two questions:

1. What are my strengths (what am I excellent at doing)?
2. What are my weaknesses (what could I benefit from developing)?

Use the following chart as an example to help visualize your outcome.

Skills and Behaviors	Strength (area to leverage)	Weakness (area of opportunity)	Action Steps
Accounting	O		Attend seminar
People skills		O	Hire someone to make phone calls
Communication skills		O	Hire a coach to assist me in managing this area
Detail work	O		
Report Analysis	O		Read Report Analysis: Level 10

Self-awareness is essential if your goal is to gain insight about your environment, the people in your environment and yourself. You must know who you are in order to run your business from a position of self-knowledge and strength. There must be a discipline of self-control working for you as you work within your system. You must maintain a process of self and business discipline to be more effective at growing your business, increasing sales and expanding your customer base.

Know Your People

The Bible says leaders should *know, nourish, lead* and *help* their people. To *know* is to understand, to *nourish* is to encourage and develop, to *lead* is to show the way and to *help* is to show care and support. If anyone on your team is disjointed, the entire team is disjointed. Work to understand the individual needs of team members—their weaknesses, strengths, learning styles and ability to handle stress. Without knowing your team members as individuals, the true potential of your people and your business will never be realized.

Knowing the answers to the following questions will help you know your team in a warmer, more business-friendly manner:

What are my team members'

o   career aspirations?
o   birthdays?
o   wedding anniversaries and spouses' names (if married)?
o   children's names and interests (if they have children)?
o   interests outside of the office?

Know your people to get the best from your team.

Know Your Vision

You should be known for your vision, a statement of purpose indicating what you are building and where you are going. Vision brings hope, focus and passion, catapulting your team towards innovation and action.

Where there is no vision the people perish.
Proverbs 29:18[26]

Write your own vision statement. Review the following vision statements of some well-known organizations:

Avon: "To be the company that best understands and satisfies the product, service and self-fulfillment needs of women—globally."[27]

Toyota (Global): "Toyota will lead the way to the future of mobility, enriching lives around the world with the safest and most responsible ways of moving people."[28]

Nike: "To bring inspiration and innovation to every athlete in the World."[29]

Know your vision to guide yourself, your people and your business through the waters of opportunity.

You Get What You Expect

If you expect to win or lose, you are right in both cases.
Elton Pride

When presented with an opportunity or task, do you expect to win or do you expect to fail? How you answer is pivotal, because your outcomes depend on what you expect. Maybe you have no expectations at all. I said this was pivotal because **you get what you expect**. If you expect nothing, you'll get nothing. If you expect to win, you will work toward winning.

The Self-Fulfilling Prophecy is a concept attributed most notably to Columbia professor Robert Merton. The theory is when you set an expectation, accurate or not, you tend to behave in a way consistent with that expectation, resulting in the expectation coming true. For example, if you set an expectation of failure ("I'm going to flunk the test"), you behave in a way that produces failure ("so why study, I'll just watch Seinfeld reruns instead; see, I flunked"), even though you were capable of succeeding.[30]

Realize this—**if you start behaving according to your expectations, you are creating your own reality—good or bad**. Give your mind directions and it will assist you in being whatever you want to be in business or in life—a WINNER or a LOSER—YOU choose.

Here's a question for you—What competitor is preventing you from achieving your goals on a daily basis, attaining more sales and increasing your network? A poem by Edwin L. Sabin reveals the answer.

> *An enemy I had, whose face I stoutly strove to know,*
> *For hard he dogged my steps unseen, wherever I did go.*
> *My plans he balked, my aims he foiled, he blocked my onward way.*
> *One night I seized him and held him fast, from him the veil did draw, I looked upon his face at last and lo ...*
> *MYSELF I SAW.*[31]

You can be your own enemy or advocate. It is not important that I believe in you. It may help. What matters most is YOU must believe in YOU. It's all about the BUSINESS OF YOU.

Taking Flight

Birds are born to fly. They migrate thousands of miles annually on a demanding, dangerous and exhausting trip, filled with risk and potential for failure. Birds use internal guidance, external markers and other birds for navigation. They make the journey because their hearts and minds have **painted a picture of success** that overrides all fear.

Like birds, you are also born to fly, and your flight begins and ends in your mind and heart. YOU can listen to your internal compass, obtain external insight and surround yourself with individuals to help lighten YOUR journey's load. Despite risk and potential for failure, you must be dedicated to your desired outcome. Unfaltering commitment will help you overcome doubt and fear. Take control of your thoughts and don't allow them to wander. Focus and discipline sharpen self-control (strengthening character) as you journey to your future place of life and business success.

As the physically weak man can make himself strong by careful and patient training, so the man of weak thoughts can make them strong by exercising himself in right thinking.
James Allen[32]

Winning Expectations—*Visualize* Positive Results

Despite naysayers and roadblocks, expect to win and never give up. Control your attitude and the choices you make to move forward with your objectives. YOU are responsible for creating the economy that will allow you to sustain you and for having the vision to see your end results.

Believe that you will succeed, and you will.
Dale Carnegie[33]

When I started as a runner, I decided very early on I would be a hurdler. As I shared this vision, some people discouraged me because I had the body and height of your average sprinter. My coach suggested another race would be more suitable for me. However, **I had a picture in my mind of being successful at hurdling**. The coach and I agreed I would work on what he felt was right for me (*not* hurdles) and he would give me time at the end of each practice to develop my hurdler skills. Over time, my coach began to notice my hurdles progress and started incorporating hurdles into my standard training. As it turned out, I *was* a hurdler, a good one, capturing two state championships in the 330 Intermediate hurdles. I continued to stand out as a college athlete.

Having a **vision** was a **huge contributor to my hurdling success**. Vision is being able to see what others cannot or refuse to see.

Webster defines the concept this way:

> **Vision** is: *the act or power of imagination, mode of seeing or conceiving, unusual discernment or foresight.* "[34]

My uncle *cast* a vision for me with his "If" challenge. The "*If*" became a "*when.*"

When I do it, I become it.

I believed despite all discouragement and criticism. My next step, my only way to get to my expected outcome, was **vision execution**. You need to combine **vision, purpose and execution** to transform your dream into reality. For the vision to live, someone has to execute it—YOU.

What separates the developer of a successful dream from a mere daydreamer is committed action.
John Maxwell[35]

This seems so clear, yet **many individuals end the process before executing their vision**, and they wonder why they don't have more customers or why there isn't more cash flow.

Are you wondering how **vision execution** relates to you and your business? In any business cash flow is king. To have cash flowing, somebody has to take action to encourage the **currency** current to flow into your business. Start the process by asking yourself these questions:

1. What is your business niche?
2. Who is your target audience?

3. What is your product?
4. Why should your target audience desire your product?
5. What is the outcome you produce for potential customers?

Your response will **help you better understand your business and customers**. You may have an established business and never thought about creating a niche. This activity can propel you into visualized execution and tangible results—more growth and expansion for your business in products, customers, service and new business. Increased Cash Flow!

There are strong parallels between business and athletics. As a runner, I desired to win the race (**increase cash flow**). To accomplish that I had to stretch, sweat and build the body (**grow or start a new business**). By executing a robust and flexible training plan, I closed the gap between my current athletic ability and where I needed to be (**develop and modify business plan**). I persevered and asked "why not" when I got pushback from doubters who didn't see my vision as a hurdler (**ask "why not" and go get what you want—more customers, more cash flow**).

By the way, **if you believe in yourself** you will ask for what you want—**ASK FOR THE BUSINESS.** Work toward getting what belongs to you. Business won't come handed to you on a silver platter; ask for it and work for it. The worst that can happen is you'll get turned down—this time. However, be persistent and passionate in your pursuit to increase your chances of **growing your business and your cash flow**. Doing this will enhance your business survival.

One way to remember this is the acronym CPR. **Business survival CPR** depends on **c**ash flow, **p**assion and **r**esilience.

C ash Flow

This is the lifeblood of your business; without it, you will be gasping for air and wondering how you will survive. The mistake most business owners make early on is underestimating how much money is needed to maintain the business in the infancy stage (1-5 years). Most entrepreneurs don't close their business doors because of lack of desire. It's usually because of lack of CASH FLOW. **Get the capital you need, control overall costs** and you will have a better chance of **servicing your client base for many years to come.**

P assion

If you lack passion, stop now and save yourself a lot of the time, money and heartache that accompanies running your own business. Passion **provides the drive, persistence, inspiration and energy** to keep you moving toward the outcome pictured in your mind.

The path to glory is usually through opposition. If you're not passionate about what you're doing, you are sure to quit long before you reach the glory of success. **If you want to swim in the waters of entrepreneurship, passion is a requirement.**

R esilience

Things will surely happen to try to stop your progress -- negative thoughts (wrong mindset), naysayers and competition. Getting knocked down isn't the issue. Getting back up is. **Resilience wrapped in passion (supported by sufficient capital) will drive you to get up, look up and stand on the podium of your business victory.**

Next up, how those negative thoughts (a wrong mindset), might derail you. But you can turn it around.

Discover Your Infinite Insight

Sometimes people do everything right, or think they do, and wonder why they don't reach their goals. It might be due to mindset. I've invested time and effort on mindset to move beyond the stereotyping limiting beliefs others had about me and I had about myself. As I progressed in life as a person, athlete, corporate professional, business owner and father, I realized time and **mindset** affected whether I'd move forward in a big way or just "get by."

Here's an example of the power of mindset. David, one of our clients, was told by his doctor he had diabetes; he needed to accept it and he'd be on medication for the rest of his life. David responded by saying, "Doctor, you're fired." (No, he isn't related to Donald Trump.) He followed most of his doctor's advice, but *not* about accepting a life on medication. David acknowledged he'd made mistakes with his eating habits and stepped up to a diet and exercise lifestyle change, losing a whopping 62 pounds. **How did David overcome his past mistakes and embrace a new and better life?** I'll get back to David shortly.

I'll share what mindset is and why you should use it to your advantage. We've all heard about mindset in some form since childhood: "you have a cluttered mind," "you need to have an open mind" or "you should make up your mind." I'll begin by making sure everyone is on the same page with **what mindset is**.

Webster Learner's Dictionary defines the concept this way:

> **Mindset** is: *a particular way of thinking: a person's attitude or set of opinions about something—the action of using your mind to produce ideas, decisions, memories, etc.: the activity of thinking about something.*[36]

Much of what we know about mindset (and much of what I share about it in this book) is the result of Stanford University psychologist Carol Dweck's (Ph.D.) research. Dr. Dweck adds this to the **mindset** definition—*"peoples' beliefs about themselves, beliefs about their qualities and abilities and, beliefs about whether those abilities are set or able to be developed."*[37]

Your mind reveals **your infinite insight** *or* **your limiting beliefs**—you determine which one. These come in the form of two mindsets: fixed or growth. Most of us move back and forth between the two or stay camped out in one or the other. I'll examine both mindset types to discover which one you identify with. Next I'll look at how to break free of the hidden barriers and "success stuck points" which have kept you from achieving the success you deserve in personal development, business, money and sales.

What Does *Your* Mindset Reveal?

Fixed Mindset

A fixed mindset says you can't develop or change; you will always be the way you are. When a fixed mindset makes a mistake, the inner voice might say, "I'm a loser; I'm stupid."

The only place where your dream becomes impossible is in your own thinking.
Robert H. Schuller[38]

Growth Mindset – Believing in Yourself (and others)

A growth mindset believes you *can* cultivate your basic qualities through your own efforts. The growth mindset is a starting point for change and growth. When a growth mindset makes a mistake, the inner voice might say, "What can I learn from this; how can I do better next time?" If my grandmother had not been working from a growth mindset, she would have given up on me at a very early age. She *might have* said, "Oh, he can't do any better. He's not that smart; that's just the way he is." Instead, (with a growth mindset) she believed by changing my environment she could help reshape me. My grandmother believed I had a chance and through her actions I became a believer in my future.

The concept is true with David who got the bad news about diabetes. He lost 62 pounds and got off medication after a lifetime of what he admits were unhealthy habits. David *had* been living under a *fixed* mindset—"I can't exercise, I can't change the way I eat," and so on, until he made a conscious decision to step into a *growth* mindset. David **altered his concept of himself and his ability to change** which made a healthy diet and exercise program possible. His experience shows the real strength of the infinite insight in a growth mindset.

Change your thoughts, change your life.
James Allen[39]

Now **discover if your mindset is fixed or growth**. Read Dr. Dweck's statements that follow; which do you agree with?

1. Intelligence is fixed at birth.
2. Some people are creative, others aren't.
3. You can become a world-class expert through enough practice, whatever your starting point.
4. You can change your personality.

If you agree with both 1 and 2 you are coming from a **fixed mindset**. If you agree with 3 and 4 you have a **growth mindset**.

If you agree with 1 and 3 or 2 and 4, you are coming from a combination of both a fixed and a growth mindset.

Knowledge is power and self-awareness is a huge step toward moving forward. Don't panic if your responses revealed a tendency toward a fixed mindset. An individual's mindset is not set in stone. You *can* learn from your mistakes and move away from a limiting *fixed* mind set.

Mindset Impact on Your Business

As in life and business, your mindset matters. How you think about you ("I can do it"!), your customers, your product and your employees matters in the success of your business. With a **growth** mindset you position yourself and your business for growth. Your business should continuously move and grow in the direction of your plan. If you hit bumps in the road, the growth mindset business owner is more likely to adapt, see the opportunities and bounce back quickly. He or she might reflect on—"What can I do better or differently to be more successful?" If you find negative thoughts creeping in you must *renew your mind*—control and replace negativity with thoughts of growth. To maintain a growth mindset you must consistently *renew the mind* and *subdue the body*. The growth mindset emphasizes adapting and creating planned change and change on the fly. These are necessary elements of running successful businesses today.

Managing your business from a **fixed** mindset may not grow your business the way it should. Fixed mindsets are not willing to change and believe individuals lack the capacity to grow ("I tried, I failed."), develop or change. This perspective will hinder business growth; your business will not be positioned for change in the short or long term. Today's customers demand businesses stay current, consistent *and* change rapidly, reflecting new customers' desires; customers will take their business elsewhere.

To be transformed you must renew your mind.
Paraphrased from the Bible: Romans 12:2[40]

Familiar Treasures – Shifting Your Mindset

As a youngster I helped my grandmother maintain a garden, churn butter, make soap from fat over an open fire, preserve okra and freeze collard greens. I remember having one dish, collard greens, almost every day. We had collard greens so often I told my grandmother I was tired of eating greens. She calmly said, "Elton, you better be glad you got greens to eat." When my grandmother prepared breakfast she always cut bacon strips in half so, when I was old enough to cook I cut them in half too. I thought, "I'm learning how to be thrifty, making the most of what I have, and by saving now I'll have something for tomorrow."

Being frugal and appreciating what we had, had become necessary if we were to survive. Thriftiness had **become a kind of familiar treasure for me**. It had gotten us through the moment but oddly, it would hold me back later. **How could a once familiar treasure become a weakness in a different moment**?

Fast forward to my college years. During summer and Christmas breaks I worked for Exxon. We traveled up and down the Mississippi, Ohio, and Kanawha Rivers on vessels with five- to 12-person crews. Vessels with crews of 12 or more were assigned chefs to cook three meals a day. Once, I was responsible for cooking breakfast on a five-person vessel—captain, pilot, engineer, first mate and deckhand. I felt very proud of my biscuits, grits, eggs, bacon and coffee breakfast creation. When the captain sat down to eat the first thing he said was, "What happened to the bacon?" I had cut the bacon slices in half, just like my frugal mindset guided me to do.

Everyone knows when bacon cooks it curls up, so half a piece of bacon is a mini bite. The captain said, "Son, this is a good breakfast, but when you cook the bacon tomorrow, don't cut it in half. We got over 20 boxes of bacon in the freezer. You must have learned this conserving from someone who taught you how to survive tough times. Don't forget that. However, you also have to recognize when you are in a place of abundance; **you have to get in rhythm with the moment in order to take advantage of your new-found treasure.**"

It was a great lesson for me. I had been rooted in a belief to be thrifty no matter what, but circumstances had changed. Frugality, to the degree of my insistence, no longer applied and was holding me back. It's a good idea to save to prepare for the future. However, you must also recognize abundance and enjoy it while you can. A simple conversation with the captain began a **positive mindset shift** for me as I navigated through college and beyond. Always be aware of your mindset *and* changing conditions; capitalize on your present place of assignment to benefit you and those around you. Even thoughts about something as simple as bacon could impact your life and **success in the moment.**

Are familiar treasures holding you back? Sometimes it takes an outsider to see things objectively and **expose opportunities you may be missing due to familiarity**.

Follow these **3 steps** to move away from a *fixed* mindset, toward a *growth* mindset.

3 Steps to Developing a Growth Mindset

1. **Increase Your Knowledge**

   Embrace learning and expand your gray matter. Being a lifetime student is essential for a growth mindset and there's so much variety today—in class learning, seminars, webinars, webcasts, or simply visit your local library. It's your choice.

2. **Practice, Practice, Practice**

   Work whatever you are looking to master. Don't just practice but practice perfect. It won't help to practice doing something *incorrectly*. Perfect practice will result in a perfect performance. You might be the worst bowler on your team. If you put the time in to improve, you could become your team's strongest player.

3. **Become a Forward Failure**

   John Maxwell calls it "Failing Forward."[41] Everybody makes mistakes. Learn from them. Make your missteps stepping-stones to your next victory. When asked about his failed attempts, Thomas Edison reportedly replied, "I didn't fail 3000 times. I found 3000 ways not to create a light bulb."[42] How many ways have you failed not to create a light bulb of success in your life or business? If you missed a *eureka* moment 3000 times, now you know 3000 ways not to proceed before reaching your *Edison moment*.

There are no secrets to success. It is the result of preparation, hard work, and learning from failure.

Colin Powell[43]

Mindset and Monetary Value

Having the right mindset affects everything, like the Big Three, your wealth, health and joy in life, to the relationships you develop (or do not develop). **Mindset and MONETARY VALUE are closely linked.** I spoke earlier about how time has value and *time is money*. **How you think about time can affect your value, the value of your business and the money you make.**

For example, when someone hires you to do a job they are paying you to solve a problem. Neighbors ask you to rake their yard because they don't have the time. You charge them $20 to solve their problem, and it takes you an hour to do the job. Time spent raking the yard (solving their problem) generated twenty dollars of income. If you reject their problem (turn down job raking opportunity) the hour would result in a loss of $20, *unless* you have another opportunity to **generate something greater**—a bigger problem to solve. When you go from yard-raker to landscape architect, **your time compensation skyrockets** because the **problem solving skyrockets**. Your time compensation just went to an Edison moment.

Therefore, how you think about TIME matters—

o   What is your value?

o   What do you bring to the table?

o   Most importantly, you must answer this question for your customer:
    What is the outcome they are looking for?

What YOU Think About YOU

Everything you do is based on how you think about you and what you think you are capable of doing *at that moment*.

The battles you have in your mind are just the beginning if you have a limiting mindset saying you cannot accomplish something. Do you think you have the ability to grow and develop—to accomplish a task, to make a sale, to land a new client, to expand your business? Your mindset, your belief you can or cannot do it, makes all the difference in the world. YOU are the beginning and the end of the results YOU will get, based on how YOU believe things will turn out. The reality is **YOU are the key to YOUR success.**

Life's a Stage

The drama of life is a psychological one in which all the conditions, circumstances, and events of your life are brought to pass by your assumptions.
Neville Goddard[44]

How do you see YOU as an individual and in your business? You control your assumptions about you on the canvas of your mind. Be aware of your power and create the visual and mental set design of your mind's personal stage. Every time you step on stage to assume your role, you will get better and better until you reach your desired outcome. Form assumptions that you already are what you hope to be (in your mind) as a businessperson. You may think you have the right mindset and are already doing this; yet, things still do not work out for you. If that's the case, do the following to check your performance:

1. Whose problems are you solving?
2. Reevaluate your cash flow—where is it coming from?
3. Determine why you missed your target.
4. How did you see the outcome before you started?
5. Obtain feedback from a trusted source.

Make the necessary adjustments based on all of the above.

Author Gregg Braden put it this way:

> We live our lives based on what we believe. When we think about the truth of this statement, we immediately recognize a startling reality: Beyond anything else that we may actually do in our lives, the beliefs that precede our actions are the foundation of all that we cherish, dream, become, and accomplish.[45]

Your stage of opportunity already exists. Here's the *secret*: **realizing you must decide what portion of the existing opportunity you will allow into your life**. It's all up to YOU based on the concept you have of YOU. You can change your clothes, change a frown into a smile *and* you can also change your level of success to one of greater success: better relationships, improved sales and increased income. It all starts and ends with how YOU perceive YOU and the picture you painted on the canvas of your mind.

> He who cannot change the very fabric of his thoughts will never be able to change reality, and will never, therefore, make any progress.
> Anwar Sadat[46]

Chapter 3—Points to Remember

1. Have winning expectations.
2. Paint a visual picture of success.
3. Your mind reveals your infinite insight or your limiting beliefs.
4. A growth mindset encourages increase.
5. You can learn from your mistakes and move forward.

Ready to Take Action?

Be a believer in YOU

Make this transformation now!

Go to www.prideglobalmgmt.com/5secretsdownload3now

To download a form on: Believing in YOU

Chapter 4
Take Advantage of the Good and the Bad

Opportunity is all around us; are you aware of it and taking advantage of it as it presents itself to you? You don't want to hear these words, "opportunity passed you by," because you didn't see it. However, opportunity may not always be there; you may have to create it by changing your environment.

I will prepare and someday my chance will come.
Abraham Lincoln[47]

One day I was walking through the Atlanta airport when I noticed an *Accenture* advertisement with this quote,

Opportunity doesn't always arrive gift-wrapped.[48]

This quote was below a photograph of a polar bear on an iceberg looking at a fish encased in a block of clear ice. The ad reminded me that **opportunity is often camouflaged as disappointment**—loss of a job, position, big client or even love. However, it's how you view the situation and react to it that determines the results you get.

Think about **your block of ice**—what *gift* has arrived for you encased in disgust, worry, fear or pain? Make the best of whatever opportunity or obstacle you are dealing with in your business or personal life. Is your **self-talk** encouraging or discouraging? Every yesterday is a stepping-stone and tomorrow you get to start over with a mindset shift to stay on track toward your desired outcome. Don't concern yourself about past mistakes unless you can benefit from them.

The key to success is giving it all you've got and being in rhythm with your cash flow current. You may remember the Lombardi quote at the book's beginning. It bears repeating:

> *The price of success is hard work, dedication to the job at hand, and the determination that whether we win or lose, we have applied the best of ourselves to the task at hand.*
> *Vince Lombardi*[49]

Be Prepared for *Camouflaged* Opportunities

One of my jobs in corporate America was working as a field district manager. I was brought back in to work at the headquarters office. The understanding had been I would replace my reporting director at headquarters when the director moved on. That did not happen.

My reporting manager was great; we had an excellent relationship of learning and innovation. One day, he was told he would be moving on and another director, *not me*, would replace him. The present director told his boss he was disappointed I would not be replacing him because that was the understanding we all had. My director explained they had to find a place for another director who was being moved from his current position.

I was deeply hurt and disappointed but pushed it aside. Before the new director arrived, I implemented a process that had always worked for me to stay focused on my purpose and long-term outcome. Here is the **five-question process I continue to use; it has never let me down:**

5-Question Process

1. How can I help this individual achieve his or her outcome for the department or company?
2. What can I learn from this person (what is his or her expertise)?
3. Why am I here?
4. What aspect of his or her skill set or personality can I borrow to help me now or later?
5. When will I know I have what I need?

Did you notice there was no negative self-talk? I reminded myself of what I wanted the future to be, and began acting in a present and future-focused manner; I subdued the body and renewed the mind, having them respond to a future moment (positively) *not* a present situation (negatively). It worked! Now I cannot say there were *no* negative thoughts. However, I had to control my thoughts, just as we discussed in Chapter 3.

As I implemented my process of giving and receiving, the new manager asked me to attend a Dale Carnegie course. If I'd had a negative outlook—"Why is this happening to me, I deserved that position, I won't be sharing my knowledge with you (new director)," my Dale Carnegie course results would **not** have been possible. The outcome was phenomenal. I received Dale Carnegie's most outstanding award and I met an old friend who introduced me to the instructor. The three of us started a mastermind group which created the foundation for the business I have today.

I prepared for my next move, equipping myself where I was (in my present position) and learning all I could in the Dale Carnegie course. The process allowed me to learn from dynamic people who had been places I'd never been. I benefited from their expertise, savvy and ideas by being open to learning. **I was in a place of dissatisfaction, but I worked on my future, which produced hope.** Dissatisfaction turned into satisfaction. When I came out the other side, we all had a big win. When I was promoted to my next place of opportunity, I continued to give and receive, equipping myself for the journey I am on now.

Change always comes bearing gifts.
Price Pritchett[50]

I still use the five-question process today, with a few tweaks, for my clients. It helps them create a plan for reaching their desired outcomes.

5-Question Process—Entrepreneur Format for Clients

1. How and why should I help my clients achieve their outcomes for their department or company?
2. What do I need from my clients to help them increase their expertise?
3. How and what can I learn from my clients to help them achieve their outcomes?
4. What aspects of their skill sets or personality may be hindering their success or desired outcomes?
5. How will they know they have made the transformation they desire?

We've all circled the same mountain several times because we refuse to accept what we were meant to **learn right where we** are. Embrace every moment, as my high school teacher would say, because you have to be there anyway. You might as well get the most out of the experience and leave the mountain equipped to move on to your next mountain of opportunity. Boots Garland, one of my coaches at LSU, put it this way:

> *If you are not willing to take it to the bank now in this moment while at practice, when the time comes to make the withdrawal during the last 100 yards of the race, you will not be able to make the withdrawal you need.*

Receptivity—It's a Good Thing

I had been open to giving, listening and learning from others. This receptiveness has brought me many life-changing opportunities. I may not always agree, but I do listen, going back to my Uncle Buddy's suggestion of running around the block to develop my running skills. What if I had told my uncle I didn't have time for that and I wanted to hang out with my friends? Remember, time equals money. What would I have lost in monetary terms? (The scholarship money alone was huge.) I was a kid, a kid being teased by friends for running in circles. I might never have enjoyed the education, athletic and other success I have today. **My reaction to one comment in one moment changed my life.**

Have you ever been in a similar situation? Has anyone given you advice, feedback or even criticism you fluffed off or didn't listen to? Consider what you could have done with just one comment in a single moment to change your life. You don't realize the impact at the time. It's possible something someone says in passing could be the missing piece of the puzzle to take you to the next level.

How receptive are you to advice and feedback?

o   Do you appreciate others' ideas or do you get defensive?

o   Do you have open or closed, friendly or hostile, body language?

o   Do you make it easy or difficult for others to provide feedback?

o   Do you accept suggestions willingly? Are you open to others' insights?

o   Do you accept that people have your best interest at heart?

After heightening your receptivity, filter the feedback and influence of others by using your **selection filter**. Keep what will propel you in a positive direction and release what will hold you back. Store the information in your metaphysical backpack of life for present or future use. Author J.R. Miller plainly illustrates the need for a tool like the selection filter.

> *There have been meetings of only a moment which have left impressions for life, for eternity. No one can understand that mysterious thing we call influence ... yet every one of us continually exerts influence, either to heal, to bless, to leave marks of beauty; or to wound, to hurt, to poison, to stain other lives.*[51]

Let me be clear; feedback is essential. Simply use good judgment with it. Your role is to use the selection filter to verify how you or your business can benefit from the feedback now and in the future.

Capitalizing on Opportunities

Are you capitalizing on all the opportunities available to leave your customers with impressions that will affect them for a lifetime? Have you overlooked opportunities to create a more powerful impact? Check what you are doing against the list below. Are you:

o   Understanding the true needs of your clients?

o   Anticipating clients' wants before they know they need them?

o   Realizing the true value of a customer (long term value)?

o   Leaving customers with an experience they can only get from you?

o   Solving customers' problems?

o   Creating a picture of success for clients?

o   Increasing your knowledge base?

Leverage any **opportunities to enhance your soft skills**. Soft skills such as how you communicate, how you interact with people and how you maintain a network are critical to the development of your business. These skills are needed to showcase your special gifts. Share them with others and be a problem solver. What does all this equate to? CASH FLOW!

More Opportunities

Duality of Victory—Seeing the Now and the Future

I received a note from Mike Jones, business owner and author of numerous books, including *Unreasonable Possibilities*. Jones had this important message, "In order to be more successful, you must see the world simultaneously as it is and as it can become."[52]

Concurrently live in your current reality while seeing your future reality. Your present reality might be a negative environment filled with hurdles (as it is). However, you'll be able to manage that present a lot easier if you *create your own economy* and work to produce positive outcomes, moving toward success (as it can become).

I can apply Jones' concept to my early years as an athlete. There were **always obstacles**, me included, and people standing in my way who told me I'd have to go through them if I wanted victory. **Then I'd have a decision to make.** Would I let those problems prevent me from achieving victory, or would I **embrace my reality** and bridge over, around or through any obstacles blocking my path to victory? For me to step onto the wrestling mat, football field, dojo floor, 400 meter track or stay in college I had to make a conscious decision to **see the current obstacles as future opportunities.** I viewed victory in a broader context—as a much larger gain. I chose NOT to stand on the sidelines, only to wonder what victory might feel like.

By simultaneously living in this world with its difficulties and obstacles, and at the same moment living in your world of victory, you can see the possibility for success and triumph. The moment you rest and linger in the world of reality (as it is) of "I can't, it's too tough, I have no money, no one likes my ideas," is the moment failure begins to set in. Don't pitch a tent and camp out in valleys of disappointment, just keep moving. **Do whatever it takes** (within legal bounds) **to reach your reality of victory.** Never let anyone stop you from chasing and catching your dream.

Once you have adopted this concept, never go back to the old way of thinking. Your ability to live in these two worlds will help you feel successful when inevitable challenges occur. Be determined in your awareness of current obstacles and future victories—you must believe you already have a successful business or will add that new client. Be thankful for the results you are looking for **as if you already have them**. Be persistent, bold and fearless in your pursuit of success.

Here are five steps to assist you in your **duality of victory:**

1. Walk through the valleys; don't camp out and stand on the sidelines.
2. Know the facts—your reality—but live out your expected results.
3. Plan your path to victory; move swiftly through your hurdles.
4. See obstacles as opportunities.
5. Renew your mind and subdue your body; expect victory and you will be victorious.

Every adversity, every failure, every heartache carries with it the seed of an equal or greater benefit.
Napoleon Hill[53]

Chapter 4—Points to Remember

1. See obstacles as opportunities; break through your blocks of ice.
2. Be open to feedback, filtering it before acting on it.
3. Optimize all opportunities with current and potential customers.
4. Don't get stuck in the current reality of struggles and challenges.
5. Live in the duality of today and the future world of victory—envision your success.

Ready to Take Action?

Experience the opportunities that await you

Make this transformation now!

Go to www.prideglobalmgmt.com/5secretsdownload4now

To download a form on: Discovering Opportunities

Chapter 5
MOVE
Make Things Happen
Work Your Plan

*In preparing for battle I have always found that plans are
useless, but planning is indispensable.*
Dwight D. Eisenhower[54]

You may have concerns, negative thoughts or **self-doubt**, about **executing your vision**. However, when you know in your gut something is right for you, move forward with your plan with gusto to make it happen. Deeply rooted dreams are worth the sacrifice, even when those around you say, you can't start a business, get that promotion, win that election, or even, be a hurdler. Be courageous and go for it.

Start where you are and with what you have. It's your only starting point. Embrace it and use it as a platform to launch the new you. If you think about it, to get out of bed and start your day YOU had to do something—execute. The sooner you start *doing*, the closer you will be to closing the gap of where you are in your business and where you would like to be.

The difference between a company and its competitors is the ability to execute.
Larry Bossidy and Ram Charan[55]

Tangible results demand conscious effort in the planning stage. ***Plan*, *Act* and *Adapt*** are the **three crucial steps** I've followed to **successfully make things happen in the execution stage.** I'll cover each in detail.

Plan

Act

Adapt

Develop Your *Plan*

Let's take a look at **how to create a plan**, on a large or small scale.

o   Define what you want to accomplish and why.

o   Describe your goal(s).

o   Create action steps to achieve your desired outcome.

o   Establish a circle of support.

o   Execute your plan.

The key lies in creating a plan and then following through on it—making it happen.

Increase Your Business—Start Planning Now

Think it and make it happen.

It is the focus of the prepared mind which forges ahead.
Elton Pride

To make things happen you need a plan—a set course. To develop what you have discovered **requires** a plan. My passion and desire for more and getting closer to my desired end has always driven me to do these five things in the Planning stage:

1. Write down in descriptive language what I want.
2. Write down why my desired end is important.
3. Write out a simple plan around the idea on how to obtain my goal.
4. Study the plan and determine how to measure success.
5. Schedule time in a planner with initial action steps and get started.

How do you know how to plan and schedule? See in your mind's eye where you would like to go (the outcome you desire) and chart out how to get there—close the gap. That is your role as the bridge figure, as explained in Chapter 1.

Start with what you will do over the next two weeks, and then work out what you need to do over the next two months, six months, projecting out over the next two years and more. Your success will depend on proper preparation, planning and appropriate execution. As you look at the word *develop*, you can see how developing a plan can help in many ways.

The Merriam-Webster online dictionary says to **Develop** is:

- *To set forth or make clear*
- *To make visible or manifest*
- *To make active*
- *To promote the growth of*
- *To make available or usable to move from the original position to one providing more opportunity for effective use*[56]

Don't be afraid to be yourself and to make a few mistakes. Ask for help from peers, colleagues and mentors. If you are a perfectionist, don't let *analysis paralysis* slow down your development process. Focus on the important stuff (what will make you money) and accept your plan as is, realizing it will be tweaked along the way. Trying to come up with the perfect plan is simply a waste of time. Go with what you have.

Some Pre-Implementation Advice

I often hear people talk about how they try to make things happen in the corporate and business world. They work hard on things like ideas and proposals but never seem to enjoy success. My question to them would be, "Have you gotten into the other person's shoes and done everything possible to see the world from their perspective?" Doing that one thing—seeing things from their perspective—will help you make things happen.

Here's my story on this very topic. I was working in technology and wanted to transition over to the business side. As many of you know, this is not an easy task, and I also wanted to move from individual contributor (non-management) to manager. I felt the time was right for me and knew I would have to make it happen. I wrote a proposal, creating a new position for myself.

I held on to the proposal for a few months, waiting for the right time to present it. I finally requested a meeting with the business unit head and gave my pitch. Before the meeting I refined the proposal, based on new events and learning since creating the proposal. The Vice President seemed favorable but did not say yes or no. He simply said to give him a week. A week went by and he said give him another week. Another week went by and he said to give him yet another week. After the third week, he said I had the job—the exact job I had proposed.

My experience may sound lucky to you, but luck had nothing to do with it. I made it as easy as possible for him to say yes to my proposal by creating one from his perspective, not my perspective—What problems could I solve for him? I knew he would have to sell the proposal to someone just like I had to sell it to him. **I created the proposal as a tool for him** so he would not have to labor over anything to make it happen for him and for me. All he would have to do was figure out how to put it into his own words. I provided him with all the actual working materials he needed. I gave him tools to create a position **to solve issues he and his boss were concerned with**, which in turn solved my desire to give and receive more.

I realize now I had also **used skills and behaviors acquired from a practice of _learning where you are_**. Review the following list to help you in your implementation stage.

Skills and Behaviors

o   Sharpen your business writing skills.

o   Hone your presentation skills, especially making persuasive sales pitches.

o   Be a problem-solver, especially of other people's problems.

o   Be acutely aware of timing.

o   Establish relationships with all audience levels inside and outside your organization.

o   Recommend ideas that address the outcome your clients and organization are looking for.

o   Be patient.

Implement Your Plan—*ACT*

The whole secret of a successful life is to find out what it is one's destiny to do, and then do it.
Henry Ford[57]

Prepared Minds Forge Ahead—They Act

Nolan Bushnell, founder of Atari, has said, "Everyone gets an idea in the shower. But the successful ones get out of the shower, dry off and do something about it."[58]

Pursuing your dreams of starting your own business, producing a record, finding a cure for hiccups, etc., does not guarantee success. You must **fine tune your ability** through training, practice, hands-on experience, working with mentors and asking questions of individuals who specialize in your area of interest. If you really want to **make a difference** in your **business**, in your **community** or with your **life**, you must **commit to action** and at some point make your MOVE. *MOVE*™ is an action word:

M   **ake** It Happen

O   **rganize** Your Efforts

V   **isualize** the end

E   **xecute Your Plan** and **Enjoy** the Journey

According to Larry Bossidy and Ram Charan, **execution** is a

- ○ Discipline
- ○ Central key to strategy
- ○ Major job of the business leader
- ○ Core element of an organization's culture[59]

Several years ago, I had the opportunity to attend several training days at the Las Vegas Motor Speedway. My team and I were trained on a new vehicle being released to the marketplace in a few months. We took a break on one of the training days, and I went outside for some fresh air. I heard the roar of NASCAR vehicles going around the track, and I also heard roaring sounds overhead. I looked up and saw B-2 Stealth Bombers doing touch and go maneuvers, and this went on all day long. I finally realized that everyone—NASCAR drivers, Stealth Bomber flyers and my team were all working their stuff, perfecting the craft in their respective fields of expertise, by doing it over and over and over again. Make things happen in your area of know-how by continuously *working it.*

Those who work their land will have abundant food, but those who chase fantasies have no sense.
Proverbs 12:11[60]

Have you ever noticed the **words used by individuals who have decided to make a difference and take action**? These expressions rise to the top:

Do it

Do something about it

Act Now

Prepared Minds Forge Ahead

Make it Happen

What you are doing now counts

Getting ready is the secret of success

Here are just a few of those individuals who are **taking action** and **making a difference** that **I've had the opportunity to meet**.

Otis Day

Les Brown

Sway Calloway

John Maxwell

Naima Mora

Mister Cartoon

Hill Harper

Zoe Saldana

Alberto "Perlman" Perez

Sgt. Matt Eversmann   Ruben Studdard   Donnie McClurkin
(Black Hawk Down)

Doing Whatever

I will share what has worked best for me. I have always been willing to do **whatever would get me closer to my desired outcomes**, within legal and ethical boundaries. *Whatever* might mean working on reports or proposals at midnight, 2:00 or 4:30 in the morning. **You do what you need to do to make it happen and drive your success.**

Don't feel sorry for yourself about losing sleep. The driving question is **how badly do you want to grow your business or change the situation you are presently in?** Think back to all I discussed about passion. You will need that **passion** when the proposal calls for you to stay up all night or when you must drive 12 hours to meet a potential client. Whatever it is, you know THE TASK MUST BE DONE before your head hits the pillow. I'm reminded of the motto President Harry Truman always kept on his Oval Office desk: "The Buck Stops Here!" You do whatever it takes. Responsibility and accountability begins and ends with you. The writings of J.R. Miller add to our discussion:

There are too many people who try to shirk the hard things.
They want to get along as easily as possible. They have
ambition of a certain sort—but it is ambition to have the
victory without the battle; to get the gold without digging for
it. They would like to be learned and wise—but they do not
care to toil in study, and "burn the midnight oil," as they must
do—if they would realize their desire.[61]

It takes time for visions to materialize; along the way you must remain productive and persevere. Let's look at someone who did just that.

The Present and the Future

In Chapter 1 I talked about Carl Lewis, a consummate athlete and Olympic gold medalist. Lewis developed his running abilities to become an incredible sprinter. He leveraged his athletic achievement to create success in the business sector, with numerous flourishing businesses still operating today. Lewis applied the same high level of intensity to business, as he had applied to sports, to produce a positive outcome.

The Lewis experience shows us:

o   One's present situation in life does not predict one's future.

o   **Use what you have.**

o   Persistence pays off; never give up.

o   Your talent and abilities will make room for you.

o   You never really know what is possible if you just do it, work hard and keep at it.

o   Demonstrate excellence and the rewards will follow.

o   Don't let your current environment limit your success.

Your talents and abilities will make room for you too. However, you must do as Carl Lewis, Oprah Winfrey and others have done; use what you have.

Your imagination is the energy focusing your mind to achieve what you imagine you will be.
Elton Pride

Adapt Your Plan

Flex Your Plan

A step in the wrong direction is better than staying on the spot all our life. Once you're moving forward you can correct your course as you go.
Maxwell Maltz[62]

Don't feel *married* to your plan. Once you have a plan, be ready to change it. I worked for a large corporation for twenty years, and a major lesson I learned there was planning is essential, but it's the simple small changes in your plan that drive long-term growth. Many years ago, I learned to sail. I also discovered very quickly if I didn't change with the wind, the wind would surely change my disposition. Whether tacking up wind or yelling "jib" to alert crew members the mast was coming their way, I needed to change the way I was doing things, and I needed to do it fast. Big time flexing!

Adjust Your Speed

In 1979, Ted Turner, American media mogul and experienced yachtsman, competed in the *Fastnet* Yachting race off the coasts of Ireland and England. Weather conditions turned severe with 70-mile-per-hour winds and 50-foot-high waves. Twenty-three yachts sank or were abandoned and 15 people died. In all of that chaos, Turner won the race. When interviewed after the race, the 43-year-old Turner spoke about his strategy, "We kept going at full speed during the height of the storm." When asked if he was afraid, since 15 people had died, he added, "Yes, but I was more afraid of losing than I was of dying."[63]

Getting Unstuck in Stormy Weather

When your storm comes, will you be ready to adjust your plan on a dime and move **full speed ahead** (like Ted Turner) to achieve your objective? **Create opportunity from adversity.** Take your life off autopilot and rethink your role. Perhaps you are *stuck* in a storm right now, afraid of what lies ahead, or perhaps you are complacent and comfortable with where you are. You could be your own worst enemy if hindered by fear of change and never allowed to reach your full potential. Does your inner true self have the courage to stand up and fight, or will you simply make minimal efforts and then say, "I'm done," and give up?

The fact is change is here to stay. It's your decision whether you choose to sail or sit it out on the dock. Choose sailing and those stormy conditions may become leveraged opportunities— springboards to your next challenge and future rewards. **Champions aren't born out of sunny days** but out of adversity on stormy days when there's hardship, misfortune, risk and maybe even danger. When the storms are over, champions are able to say with confidence, "Win or lose, I gave it my all. I did my best and I never gave up."

Create Opportunity from Adversity

(left) Master Takashina 8th DAN, Me and (right) Master Yaguchi 8th DAN

Adversity reveals both strengths and, especially, weaknesses, in our foundation. Great athletes, even those prepared for change, look for ways to make their foundations even stronger. You see this in the martial arts where practitioners seek to mitigate their weaknesses and build on strengths by developing stronger foundations through training.

As a 30-year practicing martial artist, I've observed several parallels between the two disciplines of business and martial arts.

o   Martial artists create opportunity by closing gaps and creating openings to cause injury to the opponent. Fusion of mind, body and strength working as one create a foundation of balance to move seamlessly from one place to another. There's a lesson in that. To create opportunity you have to see strengths and weaknesses and close the gap, despite any fear. The gap is always from where you are to where you want or need to be. Your role is to step up and do what needs to be done. There will be opposition; your target will attempt to elude you. However, your objective is to close the gap, doing whatever it takes to reach your goal and claim victory.

- o   Martial artists know the secret to creating opportunity from adversity is preparation. This is true in business; many businesses prosper as others fail when times get tough.
- o   Martial artists move and strike to cause injury and create an advantage. Success in business is all about moving with all you've got to create impact.
- o   Martial artists are always working to build better and stronger minds and bodies. What changes must you make to create a better and stronger you?

Training transforms various parts of the body into weapons to be used freely and effectively. The quality necessary to accomplish this is self-control. To become a victor, one must first overcome his own self.
M. Nakayama[64]

Watch Out for ANTs

When people hear the word C-H-A-N-G-E they generally don't get excited and jump for joy. They're more likely to leap to the negative, letting fear and destructive thoughts kick in. Dr. Daniel G. Amen calls these **Automatic Negative Thoughts or ANTs.**[65] Like a knee jerk reaction, people listen to a little inner voice telling them, "I'm comfortable where I am, so why change?" ANTs can ruin a picnic and they can also ruin your chances of being prepared for change in your life or business. Sometimes our thoughts reveal hidden fears we must acknowledge and deal with to make progress. For example, if you tell yourself, "I do not have time to invest in a new business venture," you might really be saying, "I'm afraid to take a chance with my money and my time."

Don't let negative thoughts control your life. Be aware of destructive thoughts keeping you from developing or expanding your business. How many times have your self-conversations ended with, "I can't do that," "I'm not smart enough," "I can't stop …" or "I do not have enough …"? Face up to your ANTs.

Be prepared for what's ahead. Change and advance planning are the norm in business. If you embrace change, you will experience a lot less disappointment, frustration and fear when a crisis occurs. Your job is to determine what level of frustration you want to deal with and to prepare accordingly. The choice is up to you.

You are the key to a better tomorrow for yourself and those around you. Don't sink in self-pity or get lost in your greatness. What makes you different is you are willing to rethink your role, switch off autopilot and feel the wind and waves on your face. This develops champions—champions with courage, insight and wisdom. Get in touch with You. Make the necessary changes, stay true to your core values and come out the other side prepared to be your best.

If you want to know what your future will be, predict it, plan it, adjust it and make it happen. The bottom line is you get to create your future personal and business life. If you want a future different than your past, change and planning are not only helpful, they are REQUIRED. You can do this. Be the winner you've been called to be, because you are ready for this. Change is in the air.

It wasn't raining when Noah built the ark.
Richard C. Cushing[66]

Chapter 5—Points to Remember

1. Always have a plan.
2. Be flexible with your plan, adjusting as you go.
3. Leverage your stormy conditions and get unstuck.
4. Get off autopilot and create opportunity from opposition.
5. Embrace change rather than fear change.

Ready to MOVE?

Experience the fulfillment of getting things done
Make this transformation now!

Go to www.prideglobalmgmt.com/5secretsdownload5now

To download a form on: How to Execute

Final Words of Insight

I'll leave you with these closing words of encouragement.

Apply the **PRIDE™ 5-Step Process** I've shared with you—

o **P**urpose and Passion

o **R**ight Choices

o **I**nfinite Insight

o **D**iscover your Opportunities

o **E**xecute Your Plan

It will make a big difference in your life. Your *Purpose and Passion* will ignite you to make *Right Choices*, revealing *Infinite Insight* through universal appeal. *Infinite Insight* will position you to *Discover Your* unique *Opportunities* so you can adjust and *Execute Your Plan*. What power! Tap into it now and get what belongs to you. Discover, develop and fulfill your calling as an individual or business owner to **expand your customer base** and **increase your bottom line**!

Prepare to Win

If I can encourage you in any way, it would be to find the one thing that drives you and keeps you up at night *in a good way.* Essential to success in business or life is a *passionate*, burning desire to win. I didn't say *not to lose* which would require a different way of thinking. One says *what do I have to do not to lose*; the other says *what do I have to do to win.* As I grow as an entrepreneur, I keep the passion by **increasing my knowledge, practicing my trade, learning from my mistakes and**

networking with others. This keeps me in the winning lane in my business.

Winston Churchill said, "The price of greatness is responsibility."[67] What price are you willing to pay? What are you willing to give up—to expose you and your business to the next level? **Coach Bobby Knight** was asked after the Basketball National Championships in 1976, "Is it the will to succeed that you have been a great success?" "The will to succeed is important," Knight replied, "but I'll tell you what's more important: It's the will to prepare. It's the will to go out there every day training and building those muscles and sharpening those skills!" Make no mistake. Coach Knight's sage advice applies to sports, business and personal success.

Never Give Up

Successful individuals always give their best and never give up. A good friend and mentor once shared this advice with me:

Never give up. What you do now will prepare you for tomorrow. Whether you get what you want now or later, you'll always reap the benefits of your work.
Doug Carter

Choose to move forward—go back to school, build a business or enhance your leadership skills; simply keep at it and you will profit.

Always work hard and *learn all you can no matter where you are,* because:

o   Where you are *now* is your stepping-stone to your place of victory.

If your purpose eludes you, work at becoming the best at what you do—the Michelangelo, Beethoven or Shakespeare of whatever you are doing in the moment. Your work may reveal your true purpose; sometimes what you thought was your purpose was not your purpose after all. You will discover your purpose in the mining of those moments, applying all you have learned along your journey. The boundaries in your world will expand as you work. Your talents and abilities will always make room for you as long as you work hard and smart *where you are*. The process begins and ends with the choices you make. Your growth and learning never ends. It all comes together in **PRIDE™**.

Commit to Action—Make the Change NOW

It's not what you are going to do, but it's what you are doing now that counts.
Napoleon Hill[68]

You've read the book. Now what? Put it in a drawer or let it collect dust on your bookshelf and nothing will change. When you continue to do the same thing you've always done, your future is very predictable. You must be willing to *change* your approach to get a *different* result and reach your next level.

Tomorrow, you promise yourself, will be different, yet, tomorrow is too often a repetition of today.
James T. McCay[69]

If you took just one idea from this book and applied it, you would become a better business owner and your life would change. Keep in mind, sometimes we don't change until what we need to change becomes intolerable. Don't wait for your situation to become intolerable.

It is completely up to you to **MAKE THE CHANGE**. Take a **LEAP™** now:

L earn Where You Are—Learn all you can where you are now to prepare for where you are going.

E xpand Your Vision—Keep your desired end in sight.

A ccept Responsibility—Be accountable for where you are now and where you are going.

P roduce—Generate results (the desired outcome) where you are now to prepare for results at the next level.

What is the secret to success? As you see with the PRIDE™ system, 90% of the process is about dealing with the internal aspects of YOU. This is true for personal or business success. What is inside you, the good, the bad, and the ugly, eventually reveals itself to the outside world. You must have internal harmony if you want to achieve external bliss, because the external aspects of your business will always reflect your internal state of mind.

As a business owner there has never been a better time than NOW to make a MOVE. Change your future landscape by influencing your business environment and personal world. Keep going until it's done and then do more.

> *But I have promises to keep,*
> *And miles to go before I sleep,*
> *And miles to go before I sleep.*
> *Robert Frost*[70]

Take **PRIDE** in all you do.

Endnotes

Preface

1. Stanford Report, June 14, 2005, 2005 Stanford University Commencement Speech, *http://news.stanford.edu/ news/2005/june15/jobs-061505.html*, accessed April 10, 2013.

2. Theodore Roosevelt, "The Man in the Arena: Citizenship in a Republic," (Address delivered at the Sorbonne, Paris, April 23, 1910) http://www.theodoreroosevelt.org/research/ speech%20arena.htm, accessed April 10, 2013.

Chapter 1

3. Lewis Carroll, Paraphrased from *Alice in Wonderland* (London: Macmillan and Company, 1865), 14.

4. "New Survey: Majority of Employees Dissatisfied," Forbes, http://www.forbes.com/sites/susanadams/2012/05/18/new-survey-majority-of-employees-dissatisfied/, accessed April 10, 2013.

5. Dictionary.com, http://dictionary.reference.com/browse/purpose, accessed April 10, 2013.

6. Goodquotes.com, http://www.goodquotes.com/quote/walt-disney/, accessed April 10, 2013.

7. Stephen R. Covey, *The 8th Habit* (New York: Free Press, 2004), 70.

8. James Allen, *As a Man Thinketh* (USA: Barnes & Noble, 2002), 15.

9. Art of Dharma, http://www.artofdharma.org/the-true-source-of-happiness-your-mind/, accessed April 10, 2013.

10. "Sanford and Son," NBC Network Television, 1972-1977.

11. Jay Elliot, *Steve Jobs Way: Leadership for a New Generation* (New York: Vanguard Press, 2011), 15.

12. Collins English Dictionary, http://www.collinsdictionary.com/dictionary/english/passions, accessed April 10, 2013.

13. Walter Isaacson, *Steve Jobs* (New York: Simon & Schuster, 2011), 567.

14. Gregg Braden, *The Spontaneous Healing of Belief* (Carlsbad, California: Hay House, 2008), 145.

15. Stanford Report, June 14, 2005, 2005 Stanford University Commencement Speech, *http://news.stanford.edu/news/2005/june15/jobs-061505.html*, accessed April 10, 2013.

16. Proverbs 13:4, Bible (New Living Translation Version).

17. Terri Guillemets, http://www.quotegarden.com/passion.html, accessed April 10, 2013.

Chapter 2

18. Think exist.com, http://en.thinkexist.com/quotation/life_
is_a_sum_of_all_your_choices/12616.html, accessed April
10, 2013.

19. Kelly F. Zimmerman, "Entrepreneurs Offer Tips on Starting
a Business," *Wall Street Journal Market Watch*, (July 19,
2011): pages, http://articles.marketwatch.com/2011-07-19/
finance/30745813_1_young-entrepreneurs-business-plan-
livingsocial, accessed April 10, 2013.

20. Stanford Report, June 14, 2005, 2005 Stanford University
Commencement Speech, *http://news.stanford.edu/
news/2005/june15/jobs-061505.html*, accessed April 10,
2013.

21. Dale Carnegie, *Dale Carnegie's Golden Book* (Dale
Carnegie and Associates, 1979/1996).

22. n.a., "The Papers of Martin Luther King, Jr. Birth of a
New Age," (Berkeley and Los Angeles, CA: University of
California Press, Ltd., 1955), 457.

23. Maxwell Maltz, *Psycho-Cybernetics* (New York: Simon &
Schuster, 1960), 118.

24. BrainyQuote, http://www.goodquotes.com/search/Pope/
john, accessed April 10, 2013.

Chapter 3

25. John Maxwell, *Developing The Leader Within You* (Nashville: Thomas Nelson Publishers, 1993), 74.

26. Proverbs 29:18, Bible (King James Version).

27. Avon website, http://www.ca.avon.com/PRSuite/our vision. page, accessed April 10, 2013.

28. Toyota website, *http://www.toyotaglobal.com/company/ vision_philosophy/toyota_global_vision_2020.html*, accessed April 10, 2013.

29. Nike website, *http://help-en-us.nike.com/app/answers/ detail/a_id/113/p/3897*, accessed April 10, 2013.

30. Robert Merton, *Social Theory and Social Structure* (New York: The Free Press, 1968), Chapter 16.

31. R. Ian Seymour, *Discover Your True Potential* (Canada: Pelican Publishing Company, Inc., 2001), 53.

32. James Allen, *As a Man Thinketh* (US A: Barnes & Noble, 2002), 43.

33. The Dale Carnegie Page, http://www.westegg.com/ unmaintained/carnegie/carnegie.html, accessed April 10, 2013.

34. Merriam-Webster, http://www.merriam-webster.com/ dictionary/vision, accessed April 10, 2013.

35. John Maxwell, *Your Road Map for Success* (Nashville: Thomas Nelson Publishers, 2002), 34.

36. Webster Learner's Dictionary, http://www. learnersdictionary.com/search/mindset, accessed April 10, 2013.

37. Carol S. Dweck, Ph.D., *Mindset: The New Psychology of Success* (New York: Random House Publishing Group, 2006), 6, 7, 12, 48, 137. *Readers note: Interested in learning more about Dweck's work? Google Dr. Carol Dweck and you will find an abundance of information, including interviews with the psychologist herself.*

38. BrainyQuote, http://www.brainyquote.com, accessed April 10, 2013.

39. James Allen, *As a Man Thinketh* (USA: Barnes & Noble, 2002), 34.

40. Paraphrased from Romans 12:2, Bible (New International Version).

41. John Maxwell, *Failing Forward* (Nashville, Thompson Nelson, 2002), 7.

42. Wikiquote, http://en.wikiquote.org/wiki/Thomas_Edison, accessed April 10, 2012. *Readers note: Different sites identify the number of Edison's attempts anywhere from 3,000 to over 10,000. Regardless, the point is made.*

43. BrainyQuote, http://www.brainyquote.com, accessed April 10, 2013.

44. Neville Goddard, *The Power of Awareness* (Mansfield Centre, CT: Martino Publishing, 1952), 49.

45. Gregg Braden, *The Spontaneous Healing of Belief* (Carlsbad, California: Hay House, 2008), 1.

46. Steven Covey, *The 7 Habits of Highly Effective People* (New York: Free Press, 1989/2004), 317.

Chapter 4

47. BrainyQuote, http://www.brainyquote.com/quotes/quotes/a/abrahamlin135435.html, accessed April 10, 2013.

48. *Accenture Management Consulting* advertisement, Atlanta Hartsfield International Airport, viewed February 23, 2011.

49. BrainyQuote, http://www.brainyquote.com, accessed April 10, 2013.

50. FinestQuotes.com, *http://www.finestquotes.com*, accessed April 10, 2013.

51. John Maxwell, *Developing the Leader within You* (Nashville: Thomas Nelson Publishers, 1993), 4.

52. Mike Jones, "Discover Leadership Training -- Thought of the Day" (Newsletter, November 2011).

53. GoodQuotes.com, http://www.goodquotes.com/search/napoleon+hill, accessed April 10, 2013.

Chapter 5

54. GoodQuotes.com, http://www.goodquotes.com/search/eisenhower, accessed April 10, 2013.

55. Larry Bossidy and Ram Charan, *Execution The Discipline of Getting Things Done* (New York: Crown Business, 2002), 5.

56. Merriam-Webster, http://www.merriam-webster.com/dictionary/develop, accessed April 10, 2013.

57. David Zinczenko, "Maximize Yourself," *Men's Health* (May 2007): 20.

58. John Maxwell, *Your Road Map For Success* (Nashville: Thomas Nelson Publishers, 2002), 31.

59. Larry Bossidy and Ram Charan, *Execution The Discipline of Getting Things Done* (New York: Crown Business, 2002), 21.

60. Proverbs 12:11, Bible (New International Version).

61. O Christian.com, "The Upper Currents: Chapter 12-Choosing to DO HARD Things,", http://articles.ochristian.com/article17197.shtml, accessed April 10, 2013.

62. Maxwell Maltz, *Psycho-Cybernetics* (New York: Simon & Schuster, 1960), 118.

63. Geoff Colvin, "The World's Most Admired Companies," *Fortune*, (March 3, 2011).

64. M. Nakayama, *Best Karate Kumite 1* (New York: Kodansha International, Ltd., 1978), 11.

65. *AHHA Self-Help Articles Collection*, http://ahha.org/articles.asp?Id=100, March 2011.

66. IWISE WISDOM ON-DEMAND, http://www.iwise.com, accessed April 10, 2013.

Final Words of Insight

67. GoodQuotes.com, http://www.goodquotes.com/search/churchill, accessed April 10, 2013.

68. Epictrek.com, http://www.epictrek.com/Epictrek/PlanningQuotes.html, accessed April 10, 2013.

69. IWISE WISDOM ON-DEMAND, http://www.iwise.com, accessed April 13, 2013.

70. PoemHunter.com, http://www.poemhunter.com/poems, accessed April 10, 2013.

Photo Credits

Back cover photograph of Elton Pride by Denise Philip

Chapter 5, page 75 karate photograph by Tom Leeman

PRIDE Resources

You've finished the book and started a journey that you alone control. The next step you take is an important one. You're already headed in the right direction. I've developed several programs to help you as you journey forward toward your desired outcome.

Therefore,

If YOU are ready to FOCUS ON YOU

If YOU are ready to SET AN EXAMPLE

If YOU are ready to PURSUE YOUR DREAMS

The following **resources** are for **YOU**.

The PRIDE Summit

If you said "Yes" to the above questions and are looking to increase your BIG 3— Wealth, Health and Joy, you are ready to climb to the top. **This two-day seminar** takes the book to the next level of WOW. You will enjoy the **expanded stories** and have the opportunity to work through all the **self-help tools** developed from the book. After two days of self-discovery, you will be equipped to step into your call and **run your business and life better and with more passion**.

PRIDE Speaks (Keynote)

What outcomes are you or your company looking for? If you are looking to increase your customer base, sales or the joy of your team, I would enjoy giving your company, organization or church group my very best of service. You have what it takes—good products, great ideas. Maybe you've taken class after class, attended all the seminars, met with consultants, talked to all your friends and colleagues, and you are still experiencing failure or struggling to get to your next place. If so, Creating Your Own Economy is for you.

By participating in this program, you can look forward to a transformation that will DRAMATICALLY INCREASE YOUR:

- Competitive edge
- Value of YOU
- Bottom line (more sales, more profit, more money)

PRIDE, Flash POINTS, Newsletter

Discover the truth about discipline and sacrifice, the importance of leadership, the glory in the message of change and how building a business and building your life require the same skills and personal attributes that help in the development of your greatness.

The "Flash POINTS" Newsletter is no hype, just proven facts in an easy-to-understand format to help you make the most of past achievements to achieve future success. "Flash POINTS" is all about helping you attain your role in business, entrepreneurship and in personal development.

PRIDE Mastermind

Nothing feels better than knowing what you want in life or in business, taking that first step, carrying it through to the end and finally crossing the finish line. "The Feeling of Victory" coaching links discipline and diligence to produce your desired results. This **motivational and inspirational coaching program** is designed to create passion, confidence, and enthusiasm in you as a participant.

The **program objective** is to **stir you to take action** now to increase your income, unfreeze your business and boost profits, while propelling you as an individual to new heights. With this coaching program you can experience success with business and personal initiatives to produce increased cash flow, revenues and profits.

To book Elton and find out more about his programs, go to www. prideglobalmgmt.com.

About the Author

Elton Pride began his learning and athletic endeavors early in life. He grew up in Pensacola, Florida, and attended LA Kersey Elementary School (Pensacola) from first through third grade. He was promoted to fourth grade, but his very wise grandmother realized he had not mastered his learning and held him back, not in the third grade but in the second grade. Elton basically started over at a different school, St. Joseph School, a Catholic school in downtown Pensacola. At St. Joseph's he discovered learning, discipline and athletics. After moving on to Pensacola Catholic high school, Elton spent his summers working at the Naval Air Station and Corry Field, military bases in the Pensacola area.

Working summers for the military, he learned many lessons—the importance of planning, execution of plans, being on time and service to others. His new start in a new school and work for the military both played important roles in Elton's life. They laid a robust foundation for his getting into college and staying in college.

As a young adult, Elton also discovered he had athletic abilities. He began to develop that area of his life, along with others. He became a two-time state champion in the 330 intermediate hurdles at the State of Florida. After several years of hard work, Elton received several scholarship offers to Southeastern Conference (SEC) schools. He chose Louisiana State University (LSU) in Baton Rouge, Louisiana, where he received his undergraduate degree. He had a productive running career at LSU, earning a school record as a member of the mile relay team.

After Elton left LSU, he received an academic scholarship to pursue his Master's degree at Rochester Institute of Technology

(RIT), in Rochester, New York. After graduating from RIT, he went on a journey to learn about business, entrepreneurship, leadership and how they all related to the world of discipline and sacrifice. Elton understood very well everything he had been blessed with came from working hard, working smart, asking for help and having a vision of his end results. Elton is also a member of the Phi Beta Sigma Fraternity.

He spent the last 20 years of his career working for one of the world's largest independent distributors of Toyota and Scion vehicles, Southeast Toyota Distributors, LLC (SET). While there, Elton had the opportunity to receive world-class experience in all areas of business and personal development: leadership, change management, time management, finance, technology, team building, communications, coaching, and more.

Elton Pride is the Owner and Operator of Pride Global Management, Boca Raton, FL. Pride Global Management is a training, coaching and business development organization devoted to assisting small businesses and those working in the automotive arena. Elton's passion is to help clients reach their very best place of success in business and life. The intention is to transition client companies to new areas of opportunity by capitalizing on the core of their past victories. Elton works to create new successes for his clients as they transition to their next assignment, next business idea or next phase of life. His objective is to enable clients to reach their best field of opportunity as businesspersons and entrepreneurs.

Make Your Next Move NOW!

Free Strategy Session with Elton Pride
(*Value $125.00*)

Early on I said I'd give you the opportunity to determine your next move. If you are looking to make a change, book your free 30-minute strategy session with me by going to:

www.prideglobalmgmt.com/strategysession

Please note that applications for strategy sessions are accepted only if I feel I can help and as my schedule allows.